Step-by-Step Guide to Circle Time

By Jenny Mosley

A first-stop introduction to leading successful Quality Circle Time meetings for beginners and a refresher for those who want to improve their practice.

Positive Press

Positive Press

Published in 2006 by:
Positive Press Ltd
28A Gloucester Road
Trowbridge
Wiltshire BA14 0AA

Telephone: 01225 719204
Fax: 01225 712187
E-mail: positivepress@jennymosley.co.uk
Website: www.circle-time.co.uk

Text © Jenny Mosley

ISBN 1-904866-20-4

Photography by Viewpoint, Somerset

Printed by:
Heron Press
19-24 White Hays North
West Wilts Trading Estate
Westbury
Wiltshire BA13 4JT

Contents

Foreword 3

Introduction 4

How to use this book 5

Part One: Understanding the Quality Circle Time Model 7

The benefits of Quality Circle Time 7

Quality Circle Time is safe 7

Quality Circle Time is flexible 9

The structure of Quality Circle Time 12

Getting ready for Quality Circle Time 17

Part Two: Getting to Know the Model 22

Before you begin 22

Practical Circle Time Plans 24

Into the unknown 24

Getting to know you 27

In and out 30

Can I join the game? 33

A time for telling 36

Keeper of the keys 39

Things that work for us 42

Stick with it 44

Monarch of the realm 46

Stop and think 49

In my opinion 52

All change 55

Using SEAL guidance in Quality Circle Time meetings 57

How to use the SEAL toolkit for Circle Time meetings 59

Part Three: Designing Your Own Quality Circle Times 62

The skills of Circle Time 62

Writing your own plans 65

Step One 66

Meeting up 66

Step Two 75

Warming up 75

Step Three 79

Opening up 79

Step Four 86

Cheering up 86

Step Five 88

Calming down 88

Putting It All Into Practice 92

What Teachers Ask 96

Foreword

We all have our own 'light bulb' moments in our career as educators. For me such a moment was when I began to understand that there are three very different reasons for children not behaving as we want them to. One reason may be that they have not yet learned the skills that underpin positive and pro-social behaviour. Another may be that they have the skills but are not choosing to use them – because alternative choices offer them bigger pay-offs. A third reason may be that although they have the skills, and although the incentives to use those skills are in place, they are simply too hurt and distressed to make wise choices.

Quality Circle Time was another light-bulb moment for me. It seemed a magic way of addressing all three of the reasons for behaviour difficulties. The framework of Golden Rules and Golden Time provides the motivation. Circle sessions provide the teaching of the skills children need in order to manage their feelings, develop empathy, and make and keep friends. The sessions also provide the kind of nurturing environment that reduces children's distress and hurt by enabling them to share it with others and receive support.

That is why Circle Time is important in the government's approach to the social and emotional aspects of learning materials (SEAL), on which I was privileged to work. More and more teachers are using circle time routinely in their classrooms, and looking for guidance and support in how to use it well.

This book provides that guidance. It explains the benefits of circle time and takes us through the immensely helpful structure of meeting up, warming up, opening up, cheering up and calming down. It provides just enough worked examples, helpfully grouped under the SEAL themes, to give confidence to a practitioner new to Circle Time. It then leads the practitioner into the next, less scripted steps where children explore the issues that are relevant to them as a group and as individuals.

The ideas in this book are practical and realistic. They acknowledge that some circle times can feel flat or go wrong. They help us get over those humps and become ever more confident in our practice.

Enjoy the ideas... look out for the 'Bag of Power' – and have fun with the children you teach.

Jean Gross

Jean was formerly responsible for the Primary National Strategy's work on behaviour and inclusion. She now directs the Every Child a Reader initiative.

Introduction

The social and emotional aspects of health are increasingly recognised as absolutely essential to our success as individuals and communities. So much so that, in 2005, the Department for Education and Skills introduced Guidance for Social and Emotional Aspects of Learning – SEAL.

The Guidance confirms a crucial shift in our understanding of why some people seem to glide effortlessly through life while others flounder and 'mess things up'. SEAL recognises just how much of our inner and interpersonal well-being is dependent upon how well, or not, we have learned a range of key **skills**. The word 'skill' implies something significant and positive for us as educators because we know that skilfulness is never something anyone is born with. Some people may be born with an innate aptitude for something but none of us can be become skilful unless we are given two vital things. These are **experience** and **training**.

Just like any other skill, social and emotional abilities can only flourish if they are nurtured and practised over and over again. Resources like SEAL are based on the realisation that every child should be taught social, behavioural and emotional skills in the same way that they are taught reading or mathematical skills. This teaching is too essential to be anywhere but at the absolute heart of your school's curriculum.

Before each lesson, you make a series of professional decisions about the best ways to develop your children's competency and understanding. Your learning objectives will be clear in your mind and you will have planned your lesson around the best possible means of achieving them. This book is designed to show you how to use exciting strategies to teach social, emotional and behavioural skills effectively.

How to use this book

'Step by Step' will guide you through all aspects of the delivery of Quality Circle Time meetings. As you work through the chapters, you will gain a secure grasp of the knowledge and skills that are needed to plan Circle Time meetings that are uniquely tailored to the needs of your particular setting.

Part one – benefits of Quality Circle Time and the Five Steps

The Step by Step Guide to Circle Time begins with a description of the many benefits that accrue from regular Circle Time meetings.
It includes a description of each of the Five Steps and how they fit together interchangeably to meet your children's needs.

Part two – practical Circle Time plans

This section begins with advice about the best ways to introduce Circle Time. Short, three-step meetings are suggested as a 'way in'. These help everyone to settle into the routines and rituals that make Circle Time such safe, invigorating fun. A selection of five-step meetings follows – these are designed to give you experience of the range and variety of approaches that can be employed during Circle Time.

Part three – tailoring Circle Time to your own needs

The third part of the book is designed to help you become creative. It explains how to plan each stage of a Circle Time meeting and put it all together as a coherent whole. In short, you will be successfully delivering the curriculum for social and emotional aspects of learning and a great deal more as well.

It's worth the effort!

Clear structure and clarity of purpose are just two of the features that make Quality Circle Time so appealing to its many loyal practitioners. We advise you to try to work through the book in the order in which it is written. You may be tempted to skip the theoretical bits and move straight into the lesson plans, but reading the explanations carefully is essential because your understanding of the dynamics that underpin each session will be crucial when you begin to plan independently. Time and effort spent rehearsing the model will ensure that you have the experience to create sessions that will enrich your children's lives and help them to become the self-motivated, self-assured individuals whom you want them to be.

What we don't do in this book

This book is not about the whole Quality Circle Time model. Other books include our strategies for setting up rewards and sanctions systems and ways to deal with challenging and unhappy children. They also highlight the need to take care of yourselves so that you are energetic and ready for the challenges that each day brings. Furthermore, the whole model emphasises the need to ensure that playtimes and lunchtimes are properly managed so that lessons learned in Circle Time meetings are not lost and forgotten when children are outside the classroom.

The *Step by Step Guide to Circle Time* does not revisit these aspects of the Quality Circle Time model. It concerns itself solely with planning and leading Circle Time meetings that give children experience and training in a wide range of cognitive and practical skills that will enable them to achieve satisfying, motivated and successful lives.

There are many excellent books from Positive Press and LDA that cover all the other aspects of the model.

Part One: Understanding the Quality Circle Time Model

The benefits of Quality Circle Time

Social and emotional aspects of learning are a vital part of every moment of your school's practice. They underpin the attitudes with which your children approach the challenges of learning and how they 'feel' about every lesson in the curriculum. Your academic objectives may change from lesson to lesson but the attitudes that you instil will be constant throughout the school day. They inform the way in which you work together as a community and are an important feature of your success or failure as an educational establishment.

As educators, you want attentive, motivated children in every lesson. You want your children to interact peacefully and constructively with one another. Individual and communal esteem has to be high so that everyone works towards success with confidence and good humour. All of these social and emotional aspects of learning are much too important to be left to chance. They need and deserve curriculum space that is specifically set aside.

When you think about how these essential lessons should be delivered, Quality Circle Time offers you a considerable number of advantages, which are detailed here.

Quality Circle Time is safe

Many of the issues that you will want to investigate can seem difficult, embarrassing or threatening to some children. If you want them to 'open up' and discuss social and emotional aspects of learning in a productive way, you need to be certain that everyone feels emotionally safe. Quality Circle Time is carefully designed to ensure that group cohesion is strong and supportive and that all participants feel relaxed and secure throughout the meeting. Quality Circle Time has a number of characteristics that ensure that the sense of safety is steadfastly maintained:

• Structure

Every Quality Circle Time meeting is built on a Five-Step Plan. Each stage has a specific structure and leads into the next one. The first two steps prepare the ground and are used to create just the right atmosphere of enthusiasm and trust for the middle step to be constructive and beneficial. The last two steps are used to wind things down and guarantee that the meeting closes with everyone feeling positive and calm.

• Solution focused

The atmosphere of safety is further reinforced by the requirement that everyone must be constructive during meetings. Put-downs and negative attitudes are not tolerated. The objective of every meeting is to teach positive behaviours and attitudes and to raise self-esteem. All participants are aware of this rule. They can feel safe in the knowledge that they are in a circle that is interested in finding ways of moving forward and which will never resort to unkind words or recriminations.

• Pace

Quality Circle Time meetings are lively and upbeat. It is the leader's responsibility to make sure that meetings never become dreary by moving briskly from step to step and keeping everyone's enthusiasm high.

• Variety

An amazing range of teaching strategies is available to Circle Time practitioners. Some issues require directed discussion and will involve the teaching of thinking and problem-solving skills. Others can be taught using more active methods that will be described later in this book. Your children will soon realise that every Circle Time meeting is different from the ones that went before and will look forward with a sense of expectant enthusiasm for whatever you have planned.

Quality Circle Time is flexible

The Five Step model is designed to teach social and emotional aspects of learning but can also be used for school councils. Many schools also use Circle Time to teach language skills and other academic subjects. It is particularly useful for groups of less confident children who have low self-esteem and need careful nurturing. Some enlightened schools now use the model for staff meetings so that everyone in the school can benefit from its democratic and positive ethos!

- ## Quality Circle Time builds group cohesion and strengthens the individual

Circle Time celebrates signs of progress, however small, and seeks to build on success. Every child has the chance to speak and feels safe because they know they will be heard and will not be ridiculed or criticised when they express their opinions. Each individual feels strengthened and part of a democratic culture that works together to improve life for the community. This ethos of cooperation and mutual support spills over into the playground and lesson times because the skills that are learned in Circle Time can be applied to all social situations.

Quality Circle Time enhances learning

- ## Teaching learning skills

Academic success requires more than intelligence and a well-planned curriculum. It involves high levels of skill. Quality Circle Time identifies and teaches five essential learning skills, which are:

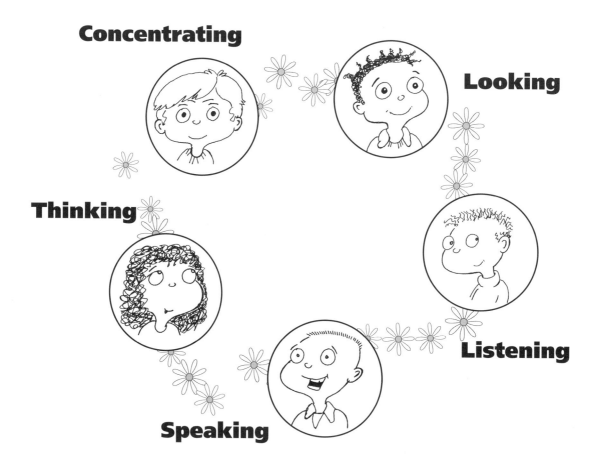

Concentrating

Looking

Thinking

Listening

Speaking

Every Circle Time meeting includes activities that encourage the development of these skills. This means that Circle Time meetings offer you academic benefits alongside their dynamic effect on social and emotional development.

The structure of Quality Circle Time

STEP 3
Opening Up Forum

STEP 2
Warming Up Round

STEP 1
Meeting Up Game

Not Heard?

JENNY MOSLEY'S 5 STEPS

Quality Circle Time meetings progress through five distinct steps. Each has a particular purpose. The theme of the meeting will be apparent in each step but will be handled differently at each stage.

STEP **4**

Cheering Up
Celebrating
Success

STEP **5**

Calming Down
Closing Ritual

Feeling GOOD!

TO QUALITY CIRCLE TIME

The two introductory steps relax the children and prepare them for the third step when key issues are investigated. The meeting draws to a close with two final steps which lighten the mood and ensure an atmosphere of closure and calm. So, the **five steps of Circle Time** are:

STEP 1

Meeting Up

Each meeting begins with an enjoyable game to help children relax, release tension and feel the joy of being together as a group. The games are designed to create a supportive atmosphere and are often used to encourage the children to sit next to those who are not their usual companions. Sometimes, you may feel that is not appropriate to begin with a lively game and may decide that a relaxing activity might be more suitable.

STEP 2

Warming Up

Many children need to 'warm up' to speaking. This is achieved through a 'round'. The teacher begins a sentence that must be repeated and completed by each child. For example, you might say, 'The animal I would like to be is ...' Each child repeats the sentence 'stem' and chooses their own way to complete it. A 'speaking object' is used to show whose turn it is to speak and whoever is holding the speaking object has the right to speak uninterrupted. (A speaking object might be a decorated wooden egg, a soft toy, 'talking teddy' or any suitable mascot.) The speaking object is then passed to the next person. Holding the speaking object does not oblige anyone to speak and any child who does not wish to do so may say, 'pass' and hand it on.

STEP 3

Opening Up

This is sometimes called 'Open Forum' and is an opportunity for children to work together to explore problems, concerns, hopes and fears. They also investigate what it means to be part of a community and think about the social and moral responsibilities that this entails. They learn how to offer peer support in respectful and compassionate ways. They practice problem-solving skills and rehearse behaviours that strengthen their confidence and self-esteem. They learn how express opinions and join in discussions that develop their ability to reason and think logically.

STEP 4

Cheering Up

It can be difficult to 'switch off' from issues of concern so it is important that you provide two closing activities that ensure everyone leaves the meeting feeling calm and refreshed. The 'cheering up' step begins this process by celebrating the group's successes and strengths and giving children the opportunity to praise one another or cheer everyone up by giving them the chance to teach everyone new skills and games.

STEP 5

Calming Down

Every meeting needs to end with a closing ritual. This winding down step is calming and ensures that a feeling of emotional safety and closure is achieved.

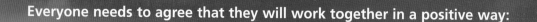

Everyone needs to agree that they will work together in a positive way:

We are kind to each other and never say hurtful things.

We know that everyone has the right to have opinions that are different from our own.

We take turns and let other people have a go.

We praise each other and thank people who have helped us.

We work together as a team

We share our opinions and learn from one another.

We think about problems and try to find solutions.

Getting Ready for Circle Time

• Find the right space

A quiet uncluttered area is an ideal base for your Circle Time meetings. It should be large enough for the children to sit in a circle, facing inwards, and engage in the activities that happen inside it. Carpet squares, cushions or chairs that show the children where to sit are helpful. It is also helpful to clear the space of anything that might distract their attention.

• Choose a good time

Circle time is important so it needs to be timetabled to reflect the value that you and your school place upon it. Choose a time when you know that everyone will be feeling energetic and alert. Stick to the timetable and never allow Circle Time to be squeezed out by the rest of the curriculum.

• Build a collection of props

Puppets are an indispensable addition to Circle Time meetings. There are books of stories and scripts available that are specially designed to use with puppets during Circle Time meetings. These will help you to become proficient enough to devise scripts of your own that meet the specific needs of your children. Many teachers also use props like crowns, cloaks and other items from the dressing-up box.

Planning is easier if you have a collection of poems and stories that can be used to stimulate drama and discussion and there are ready-made collections available. Circle Time meetings are not just about talking about difficult issues: most begin and end with a game that is designed to put the children at their ease. Party games are easy to adapt and many games from the PE curriculum can be tailored for Circle Time.

• Now assemble a 'bag of power'

Just like other lessons, not every Circle Time meeting will go as you wish. Sometimes the meetings will be flat and the children unresponsive. You will need to have something up your sleeve for these difficult moments. We call this 'the Bag of Power', a cloth bag full of Circle Time rescue remedies! Include your puppets, games and objects to intrigue and invite discussion, a book of poems, a cloak or other dressing-up clothes and a 'treasure box'. When things start to flag, just slowly put your hand in the Bag of Power and pull out something to surprise and distract. You need to be more exciting than the most disruptive child in your group so that the rest of the class ignore the distraction and focus all their attention on you!

• Prepare your adult helpers

You will need adult helpers trained to understand how Circle Time works and it is helpful to spend time before each meeting explaining what you are intending to do and what you will expect from your aides. Parents can be useful and you may decide to send out invitations so that they feel welcome to attend. This is another reason for holding your meetings at a regular time every week.

• Agree your ground rules

Ground rules tell us how to behave in particular situations. Their purpose is to minimise confusion and conflict and to create an atmosphere in which meaningful discussion can take place. To be effective, the rules must be agreed by everyone and you will need to review them before each meeting. The list below covers the ground rules that experienced practitioners find indispensable.

Everyone has the right to be heard

It is important the children have the right to be heard without interruption. This right is made very clear when a 'speaking object' is used. Only the individual who is holding the speaking object is allowed to speak. It can be passed around the group or placed in the centre of the circle and picked up by children who wish to contribute to discussions. Alternatively, children can raise their hand or do a 'thumbs-up' to indicate their wish to speak. In excellent Circle Time meetings, the teacher acts as a facilitator and skilfully ensures that children talk and debate with each other. The teacher's voice is heard less and less as children become more respectful and confident with each other. Attentive listening is a vital social skill and meetings cannot be successful if this rule is not observed. Sometimes, however, you will need to employ some polite interruption: We advise that you do so like this: *'I'm very sorry to have to interrupt you, Sally, but I need to remind Joe about one of our ground rules.'*

Everyone has the right to 'pass'

In the circle, every child has an equal right to speak. Every child also has the right to remain quiet if they so wish – they can say 'pass' if it is a round, for example. Give them another opportunity to speak at the end of each step when you can say, *'Does anyone want to change their mind and say something before we move on?'*

We are always kind and positive

Children will clam up and refuse to contribute if they feel that their views will be dismissed or ridiculed. Circle Time meetings are all about reinforcing good behaviour and it is important that only positive things are said. Participants need to be taught to make 'I' statements that describe their personal feelings so that their statements are not received as an attack. Teach your children to relate things back to their own viewpoint by using this sentence stem: 'When you ...., I felt .... '

• Facilitate different learning styles

Circle meetings are fast-paced and involve a wide range of activities. They should be designed to tap into different learning styles so that every child can excel at some point of the meeting. Shy children, for example, can be transformed by holding a puppet. Academic lessons are planned to accommodate a variety of learning styles, so plan your Circle Time activities in the same way. Both shy and outgoing children should have a chance to shine and every child must get an opportunity to learn in the way that suits them best.

• Use your adult helpers

Your adult helpers can be encouraged to give extra support where it is needed.

This may mean one-to-one support for particular children. For children whose development is delayed they can be asked to simplify tasks or they may be used to help particular children concentrate and stay on task. It is a good idea to keep an empty chair in the circle for children who find it difficult to join in. Welcome them into the circle if they choose to come in from the outside.

• Encourage, don't 'force'

Some children are reticent and are allowed to say 'pass' if they feel that they do not want to speak. They need encouragement and can be given a second chance to speak with assistance from an adult helper. Alternatively, you may find that they will feel more confident if they are allowed to hold a puppet or a cuddly toy. Be prepared to wait patiently until such children are more familiar with the routines of circle time. They will come to realise that they are in a safe environment and can trust in the people around them.

• Use the sessions to meet children's needs

If you have children in your class who display particular problems, then Circle Time is your opportunity to offer them help. For example, if you have a child who has a problem with anger then you can model and teach anger management and calming techniques. This means that the whole class learns to help one another by practising pro-active strategies and problem-solving as a team.

• Try smaller Circles of Support for 'children beyond'

Some children are exceptionally needy and cannot cope with whole-class circle meetings. These children need to attend small therapeutic meetings where their specific needs can be met. They need extra-large portions of praise and affirmation that only a small group can supply. In an ideal world, these small group meetings are timetabled to take place at the same time as the larger meetings. Children with emotional, social and behavioural problems urgently need these boosts to their self-esteem and it is well worth rearranging the timetable to accommodate them. *Running Small Circles of Support For Children 'Beyond' What Normally Works* by Jenny Mosley will be published by LDA in 2007.

Children say...

My teacher is good because she chooses good games. She thinks hard to make it fun and she works hard to be very smiley.

Fallon, Year 3

Children say...

I like holding the speaking object and talking about the things I sometimes think about.

Joseph, Year 6

Children say...

I like circle time because it relaxes me so I'm not so steamed up all the time.

Holly, Year 4

Children say...

It relaxes me so I don't yell at anyone.

James, Year 5

Part Two: Getting to Know the Model

BEFORE YOU BEGIN...

The five steps of Quality Circle Time are building blocks that join together to make a complete meeting. Jumping in and attempting all of these steps at once may be too much for your children, so we advise you to introduce Circle Time in planned stages. This will enable you to build trust and group strength so that, when everyone is ready, you can hold complete five-step meetings successfully and with confidence. We advise you to work towards full meetings in the following way:

1. Teach the five skills

It is wise to introduce a programme to teach the five skills of Quality Circle Time before you start to hold Circle Time meetings. These skills are essential if your meetings are to run smoothly with children who are alert and attentive. You can make this fun by playing simple games and by referring to the skills frequently throughout the day, by saying things like, *'Well, done, Stephen, I have noticed that you are using your listening skills very well today'*. By reinforcing the five skills you can guarantee that children understand the behaviour that will be expected of them and will be ready to focus their minds. Older children need a reminder of the five skills prior to each meeting and it is useful to teach younger children the script below:

In circle time...

We use our looking skills (point to eyes)

We use our listening skills (point to ears)

We use our speaking skills (point to mouths)

We use our thinking skills (place hands on side of head)

We use our concentration skills (clasp hands and place in laps)

The teaching of these skills can also be made into a daily 'circle ritual'. Decide on a suitable time to hold your ritual, perhaps after registration, and use this time to remind the children of the five learning skills. Make a poster-sized version of the skills so that they are visible in the classroom. You can point to the poster throughout the day as you praise children for developing their skills. Even better, if you have the energy, why not take photographs of your children using different skills. Don't leave any child out by mistake. Keep changing the display.

2. Introduce Circle Time with three-step meetings

In three step meetings the 'Opening Up' phase is omitted and the leader pick-and-mixes from the other steps to create active, exciting circle meetings. These simple meetings help everyone to become accustomed to the activities that take place during Circle Time. This is an opportunity to try out different combinations of activities from the remaining four steps. For example, game/round/game; game/ round/celebration; game/celebration/calming down; calming down/round/calming down and so on. Eventually your group will be ready to try the more difficult 'Opening Up' phase with confidence because every other step will be familiar.

You can find a range of popular Circle Time activities in this book and many more can be found in the SEAL toolkit. (A 'further reading' list is included at the back of this book.) Read through each activity or game before you play it so that you are sure that you have identified the skills it is reinforcing. While you are playing, you need to mention the underlying skill so that your children can learn to recognise how it feels in practice. For example: *'Well done, Josie, for using your looking skills so cleverly,'* or *'That game needed a lot of concentration. Thank you everyone, for concentrating so hard.'* If you don't tell them why they are playing the games, a learning opportunity will be lost.

3. Use Circle Time plans

Once you have introduced Quality Circle Time with three step meetings, you will be ready to deliver full five-step meetings. Try out the scripts that follow and you will soon be familiar with the ways things work.

Practical Circle Time Plans

The plans that follow are designed to show you the range of approaches that can be utilised during Circle Time meetings. The themes have been carefully chosen to reflect the Primary National Strategy guidance for the teaching of the social and emotional aspects of learning. Each session should take about half an hour but may take longer if the children respond well to the middle stage and you allow them to investigate the issue in more depth. However, if you decide to give more time to the 'Opening Up' don't forget that the closing steps are vital to bring the meeting to a close in an atmosphere of positivity and calm. The meetings are suitable for a wide age span, but you may need to adapt them to suit your particular group.

INTO THE UNKNOWN

SEAL theme: New beginnings

Focus: Getting to know one another

What you need: Two blankets or large sheet of cloth; a number of different objects from around the classroom – a photo, a storybook, a purse, skipping rope etc

Preparation: Spread the objects across the floor and cover them with the blanket

Meeting up

When the children are sitting in the circle, ask them to curl up with their knees touching their chests. When their name is called, they must uncurl and look steadily at you. Then you welcome them into the circle with the words:

Leader:	Where is Susie?
Susie:	Here I am.
Leader:	Great to see you. 1,2,3.
Everyone:	Great to see you, Susie.
Leader:	It's very nice to see you today!

Warming up

Give the speaking object to the child sitting next to you and ask him/her to complete the following sentence: *'My name is* (insert name) *and I like to* (insert skip, sing, play football etc)'. Continue this around the group. If some children are shy, you can prepare them for this activity by talking about it before the meeting and/or giving them a picture of their favourite activity that they can hold up. They can say, *'I **would** like to* (ski, parachute)' if they wish.

Opening up

Choose each child in turn to wriggle under the blanket and bring out an object. Ask them to show the group what they have found and to give it to someone in the group (not their best friend) who might like it. The receiver should say, *'Thank you'*. Both children can demonstrate and talk about the use of the object, e.g. *'I gave it to you because ....'* or *'I like it because.........'*

Tell the children that it can be a bit scary to go under the dark blanket and then stand up and talk to the rest of the group. Ask if there have been other times when they have felt scared and talk about ways of making it less scary. You can use sentence stems like, *'I need help because* (I get scared when it's quiet at night).' *'I get scared when* (I have to talk in front of the whole school).'* Ask them to listen to suggestions from other children about coping strategies they have found useful.

> It boosts children's self-esteem to realise that they have wisdom that they can share with others. It is important that adults sometimes share their feelings and allow the children to learn that they can help adults too.

Cheering up

Use this rhyme to the tune of 'Muffin Man':

If you've been under the blanket today,
Blanket today, blanket today,
If you've been under the blanket today,
Stand up and shout 'Hoo-ray! Hooooooo...ray!"

Calming down

Tell the children that the blanket has another use: we can wrap ourselves up in it and feel nice and snug and warm. Let the children lie with their feet all pointing into the middle and lay two big blankets over them. Say, *'You are feeling very calm and happy. Breathe in 1, 2, 3. Now, I am going to slowly slide the warm blanket away but everyone can keep the calm happy feeling. You can hold on it because its inside you!'*
Go round and tap each child gently on the shoulder and lead them quietly to their next activity.

> At other times during the day, help children to breathe calmly.

GETTING TO KNOW YOU

SEAL theme: New beginnings

Focus: Boosting the individual and strengthening the group

What you need: Speaking object; fruit basket

Meeting up

The children sit in a circle. Go around the group and label each child either an orange or lemon. Call out 'oranges', or 'lemons' or 'fruit basket'. The children in the named category must change places. When 'fruit basket' is called, everybody changes places.

> **The purpose of this game is to make sure that everyone 'mixes up' and sits next to someone with whom they would not usually interact. Explore other games that help children to sit next to 'new' people.**

Warming up

Each member introduces him/herself and physically makes one action to indicate how they are feeling now. For example, Joe is tired and so he stretches, Shakira is excited so she jumps up and down. The whole group imitates that person's contribution.

> **Work on these ideas before Circle Time and put them up on the wall.**

Opening up

Everybody should mingle inside the circle – they have two minutes to shake each other's hands, give their names and tell a fact that they think everybody knows about them, e.g., *'I like jelly sandwiches.'* The children then return to their circle seats.

> **Don't forget that adults must try to join in Circle Time activities.**

Now ask if they can remember any of the facts. Ask for volunteers to stand up and introduce a classmate like this: *'This is Kayleigh and she likes to dance to loud music in the kitchen.'* Kayleigh then introduces another person until the whole group is standing up. Ask another child to walk around the group labelling each child A-B-A-B-A-B-A around the circle. All the 'A' children should now move their chairs to face the 'B' children so that an inner and outer circle is formed. These pairs of children now have to discover three things that they **both** like and three things that they **both** dislike. When you re-form the larger circle, ask the 'A' children to introduce their partner and recount the things that they both like. The 'B' children then introduce their partner and recount the things that they both dislike.

> **The aim here is to introduce the concept of shared experience and individual differences at a basic level.**

Cheering up

Congratulate all the children on their speaking skills and highlight individuals who have displayed particular skill – for example, *'Well done, Joe, I liked the way you used eye contact.'* Or, *'Susie, the way you stood still made it much easier to concentrate on what you were saying.'* and so on.

Calming down

Ask the children to hold hands in the group and close their eyes. Gently squeeze the hand of the child next to you and ask him/her to pass the squeeze on to the next person and so on around the circle. Repeat this with a smile and then with a 'hello'. Unclasp hands and thank the children for listening to each other so well.

TOP TIP

Like Chinese Whispers, pass around a shape drawn on a palm. It doesn't really matter what is drawn – it's a lovely feeling.

TOP TIP

Take time to reflect on the success of your Circle Time. If your teaching assistant is able to join you all ask her for her thoughts on how you could plan the next meeting to embrace more children's needs. For example; if too many children say 'pass' – then a few days before Circle Time give them notice of what the sentence stem will be. They can then prepare by bringing a little card with them to remind them what they want to say. If a child is terribly shy they can give their card to someone else to read – or whisper to your puppet who can then speak for them

IN AND OUT

This circle meeting uses a game as stimulus for discussion and debate.

SEAL theme: Getting on and falling out

Focus: Empathy and our power to make others happy

What you need: Speaking object

Meeting up

Begin with a game of 'Hunter and Hunted'. The children sit in a circle and two children are chosen and blindfolded. The first is the hunter, the other the hunted. Within the circle, the hunter attempts to capture the quarry. The rest of the group sit in a circle and guide them away from the edge of the circle with very gentle contact, using palms of hands only.

This game ensures a kind, co-operative atmosphere.

Warming up

Using the speaking object, ask each child in turn to complete the following sentence: *'I like to play with* (insert name of playmate from home or school) *because* (insert reason).' Children who do not wish to speak may say 'pass' and give the speaking object to the next child.

Opening up

Explain that the following game will remind us of the good feelings we get from being part of a group, and the bad feeling we get when we are left out or made to feel different. Choose a popular, confident member of the group and ask him/her to stand in the middle of the circle. Tell the rest of the class to move clockwise, covering the seats with their behinds as they move from chair to chair (so that there is always an empty chair but it appears and disappears as the children move around). The volunteer has to try and sit on an empty chair and the class has to try to prevent him/her from doing so. When the game is over, the volunteer sits in the middle of the circle. Ask the children if any of them can identify how the volunteer may be feeling. They should come forward and put a hand on her shoulder and speak 'for' her. For example: 'You may be feeling very stupid. Everyone else was having a good time.' 'You may be feeling frustrated …'

> **This activity teaches children about empathy and can be used in many Circle Time meetings.**

If no-one mentions the idea of rejection, you can comment on how the scene looked to you as an observer. Explain how it is reminiscent of playground scenarios. Can any children describe similar situations and make a list of them? Offer a choice of sentence stem – such as 'A time when I felt left out was …' or 'Some people feel left out when …' Use the list and ask children to share strategies that they have found useful in similar situations. You may choose to support their suggestions by offering the sentence stem 'Would it help if …?'

> **Giving the children the first half of a sentence, and asking them to complete it, helps them to phrase the answer clearly and concisely.**

Cheering up

Thank the children for their useful contributions and point out that they are learning the meaning of the word *empathy*. Be specific and thank some children personally while praising the group as a whole.

(A definition of empathy is *'insight into the motives, feelings and behaviour of others and the ability to communicate this understanding'.)*

Calming down

Tell the children that you are going to show them how to calm down when the going gets tough. Explain that we can calm ourselves down by concentrating on our breathing. Show them what you mean by sitting still and quiet and letting your breath become steady and slow. Ask them to try this out. Sit quietly for a few minutes. Play a CD of quiet water sounds (from any alternative 'healing' shop). Afterwards ask them to 'thumb up' any sounds they heard when they were very quiet.

CAN I JOIN THE GAME?

This session uses a puppet script to stimulate discussion in an atmosphere of safety.

SEAL theme: Getting on and falling out

Focus: The social skills involved in friendship

What you need: Two glove puppets; a small selection of toys

Preparation: None

Meeting up

Play a game of 'Who's talking now?' The children sit in a circle and you have to choose one to be the monarch. This child stands in the centre of the circle wearing the blindfold. On the command, 'Go' the other children walk round the circle until the monarch calls, 'Stop'. She then points straight ahead and asks, *'Who goes there, friend or foe?'* The child who is being pointed at answers, *'Why, friend of course your Majesty'*. The monarch should now try to guess the identity of the speaker. If they guess correctly, the two of them swap places. If the guess is incorrect, the monarch stays in the centre and a new game begins.

Warming up

Using the speaking object, ask each child in turn to complete the following sentence: *'I like to play with* (insert name of playmate) *because* (insert reason)'. Children who do not wish to speak may say 'pass' and give the speaking object to the next child.

Opening up

Introduce the puppets to the children. We are going to call them Perry Pig and Jerry Giraffe. Play out the following script with the puppets:

Leader:	Perry, you're looking sad and lonely. What can have made you feel so sad?
Perry:	I want to play with Jerry but he won't let me.
Leader:	Jerry, why won't you play with Jerry today?
Jerry:	Because I want to play all by myself.
Leader:	But, Jerry, I thought that Perry was your friend? Friends don't make each other sad and lonely.

Ask the children what they think that Perry and Jerry should do. Take their suggestions and repeat them so that everyone is clear. Use the puppets to show the children how these suggestions might work out in practice and add some more of our own by saying things like: *'I was in the playground yesterday and I saw how Samantha joined in Kerry and Josie's game by offering to hold the rope. That was clever of you, Samantha. Perhaps some of you might like to try something like that when you want to join in a game.'*

> **Children love puppets and it is a good idea to practice at home so that you feel relaxed when you use them in the class.**

Cheering up

Ask the children to join hands in a circle and sing or chant the following rhyme. At the end of each line, they raise their hands towards the ceiling and then lower them. At the end of the last line, they let go and point to everyone else in the group with a big smile.

I'm happy with my friends
I'm happy when we play
I'm happy with my friends

And you're my friends today!

Calming down

Try a breathing exercise. Tell the children to take a deep breath while you count to four. Then, as you count back to one, ask them to breathe out slowly.

A TIME FOR TELLING

This meeting celebrates children's ability to solve problems and find solutions.

SEAL theme: Say no to bullying

Focus: Agreeing a procedure for reporting incidents of bullying

What you need: Speaking object

Meeting up

Turn to the child next to you and greet them by smiling and saying hello. Ask this child to pass on a greeting. They may do so by copying your or by changing it to a 'high five', a 'hi-ya' or any other greeting that they know. When these greetings have completed the circle, you can all try out any new ones as a group

Warming up

Using the speaking object, ask each child in turn to complete the following sentence: *'I know someone is unhappy when I see them* (crying, looking at their feet, fiddling with their cuffs etc)'. Children who do not wish to speak may say 'pass' and give the speaking object to the next child.

Opening up

Explain to the children that, today, you will be looking at the difference between 'telling tales' and reporting bullying incidents. Read out the following statements and ask the children to decide which each one is.

1) Ashley tells the teacher that Damon keeps hiding his work to try to get him into trouble.

2) Alicia tells the teacher that Mary is playing with a toy on the carpet during listening time.

3) Shaheen tells the teacher that Alice is saying nasty things about a new girl so that no-one will like her.

4) Sam tells the teacher that Daniel hasn't handed his work in as requested.

5) Rashad tells the teacher that Leroy was playing with water in the toilets.

6) Zoe tells the teacher that Cara has been calling Maxine a nasty name during playtimes.

Using examples like this makes it easier for children to identify problems and see them more clearly.

Talk about the difference between telling tales and reporting incidents of bullying. (Numbers 2, 4, 5 can be considered 'telling tales'.) Explain clearly that you are **telling tales** about someone when their actions are **not hurting anyone else**. Now ask the children why people don't always report incidents of bullying. They will probably give answers such as:

'I don't like telling tales.'
'If I tell on someone, everyone might dislike me.'
'I'm scared that the bully will pick on me.'
'The bully is my friend.'
'I don't like the victim.'

Explain that if a safe school is to be created for everyone it is important that incidents of bullying are reported to an adult. Do the children think it would be easier to report incidents if they could do this confidentially? Ask them for suggestions on how this could be achieved. For example, you may have a box in the classroom where notes could be posted, or you might have a special time and place where children could meet with you to report incidents. Before you agree a set procedure for reporting any incidents, you will need to have discussed the issue in a staff meeting. Be prepared to negotiate and take suggestions back to the rest of the staff before they are agreed.

Cheering up

Thank the children for their wisdom and insightful suggestions. Join together for a joyful Mexican wave to celebrate your strength as a group.

Calming down

Ask the children to sit with straight backs, hands resting gently in their laps. Tell them to close their eyes and to think about their breathing. Tell them that you want them to breathe in a feeling of happiness and, as they breathe out, you want them to breathe out any feelings or thoughts that may be making them unhappy. Next, ask them to think about themselves enjoying a lovely warm summer day, doing things that they really enjoy. Finally, they can slowly open their eyes and become aware of the room and the present moment.

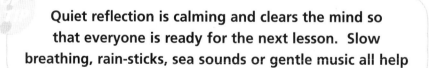

Quiet reflection is calming and clears the mind so that everyone is ready for the next lesson. Slow breathing, rain-sticks, sea sounds or gentle music all help

KEEPER OF THE KEYS

Theme: Going for goals

Focus: Encouraging children to think about what they want to achieve and what stops them

What you need: Speaking object; lots of loosely-scrunched sheets of newspaper

Meeting up

Make a circle with sufficient space for the children to move around inside. Explain to the children that they are going to walk around pretending they are on different surfaces. Start with thick, squelchy mud. At intervals, change the surface: slippery ice, a trampoline, quicksand, hot coals, glue, long grass etc.

Warming up

Using the speaking object or a wand, ask each child in turn to complete the following sentence: *'If I were a magician, I would …'* Children who do not wish to speak may say 'pass' and give the speaking object to the next child.

Opening up

Place a chair in the centre of the circle and surround it with lots of scrunchy newspaper. Place some 'treasure' (something noisy like keys or bells) under the chair. Now choose a child to be the 'guardian of the treasure'. Give him a blindfold and seat him on the guardian's chair. Select another child to be the 'seeker'. This child must try to retrieve the treasure without being caught. It is the guardian's task to listen carefully and point to the seeker and say, 'stop' loudly if he thinks he knows where the seeker is. The seeker has to freeze. If the pointed finger is in their direction, they have to return to their seat. The guardian is allowed only three attempts at stopping any seeker. If the treasure seeker reaches the treasure without being stopped, give them a clap. Next, clear everything away

and initiate a discussion about goals, which should be compared to the treasure in the game. What would we like to achieve and what prevents us from achieving these things? Some children will able to volunteer some goals and the obstacles that need to be overcome. Everyone should be given the opportunity to offer advice, using the sentence starter, 'Would it help if …?' As a follow-up, children can make individual action plans to help them reach their 'treasure'.

Cheering up

Tell the children that you have noticed some of them working hard lately, and that you are confident that they will achieve their ambitions through hard work and effort. Read out their names and the occasion when you noticed them trying really hard. Ask them to look out for examples of hard work to celebrate next week.

Calming down

Sit quietly with eyes closed and hands in laps. Read the following script slowly, leaving pauses where the dotted lines appear.

You are going to imagine that you are riding on a magic carpet which will take you to exciting, interesting places. Think of yourself lying on the carpet. What is it like? Imagine the colours, patterns and texture of your carpet …
(pause)
It lifts up into the air. You feel the wind on your face as the carpet glides through the sky. Below you is the sea twinkling and glistening in the sunlight. You can see things on the water …
(Pause)
Now the carpet is soaring higher as you approach mountains. Look down and see the snow-covered peaks, crisp and white. Feel the cold air – it makes you shiver …

(Pause)

You see a group of skiers on a snowy slope. Imagine them sliding smoothly down, twisting this way and that. You can hear the swish of their skis as they move …

(Pause)

You are past the mountains now and the carpet drops down lower. You feel the air getting warmer and enjoy the sun on your back …

(Pause)

It is now time to travel home. You lie on your back and feel the gentle swaying of the carpet, thinking of all the things you have seen on your journey.

Allow the children a few minutes to 'come back' to the classroom and then guide them quietly to the next lesson.

THINGS THAT WORK FOR US

SEAL theme: Going for goals

Focus: Investigating the children's perception of methods for motivating them

What you need: Speaking object; two identical cut-out figures, one showing a happy, smiling face, the other a sad face; scissors; blu-tack; flip-chart and pens

Meeting up

Form the circle and explain to the children that they are going to clap some rhythms. At the same time you are going to call out instructions that they must follow. For example:

Clap high (clap above your head) 1, 2, 3, 4

Clap low (clap down by your knees) 1, 2, 3, 4

Clap to the right, 1, 2, 3, 4

Clap to the left, 1, 2, 3, 4

Clap with your partner (both hands together) 1, 2, 3, 4

Warming up

Using the speaking object, ask each child in turn to complete the following sentence: 'At school, I like it when …' Children who do not wish to speak may say 'pass' and give the speaking object to the next child.

Opening up

Pin up the picture of the happy figure and choose a name that belongs to nobody in your class. You are going to tell the children about a day in the life of this child. Explain that he woke up happy and enthusiastic about going to school. Go through the day and describe how everything seems to go wrong. He gets his sums wrong, he loses his pencil, nobody will play with him at playtime, someone shouts at him. As you mention each one of these things, cut a 'jigsaw' shape out of the sad figure and stick it on to the happy figure. By the end of the day, the happy, smiling child has turned into an unhappy figure!

Make a list of the things that could be done to make him feel better by asking the children to suggest things that they like receiving – praise, smiles, stickers, stamps, certificates, peer praise, Golden Time, letters home etc. Can the children rate each of these 'motivators' out of ten, or rank them in order with the most effective first and least effective last? You might find it easier to divide the children into groups for this. The groups can share their opinions and explain the reasons for their choices. Close by removing the blue jigsaw pieces and return the sad figure to its happy, smiling state! (You might want to introduce the important concept of self-praise at this point.)

> **Self-praise is a fundamental aspect of healthy self-esteem and children should be encouraged to recognise, appreciate and applaud themselves when they have done something well. This is not immodest, but valuable self-assessment and we all have the right to be pleased with a job well done. If we know our strengths, we'll ask for help with our weaknesses.**

Cheering up
Join together with the joyful statement, 'We are all wonderful!' and do a Mexican wave. Repeat this a couple of times.

Calming down
Explain that you are the rain, denoted by waving fingers. Pass the action around the circle. Next, become the thunder and mime this by slapping your knees in rhythm. Again, pass the action around the circle. Finally, bring out the sun by folding your arms, and let this action pass around the group.

STICK WITH IT

SEAL theme: Good to be me

Focus: Developing a positive self-image

What you need: Stickers with smiley faces drawn on them; a smiling puppet or picture of someone smiling; cheerful music (eg The Dance of the Sugar Plum Fairy by Tchaikovsky).

Meeting up

Quickly mix the children with a game like 'fruit basket'. Then, divide them into pairs. They have to take it in turns to try to make their partner laugh. They can pull silly faces but must not make physical contact while the partner has to remain serious for as long as possible.

Warming up

Using the speaking object, ask the children to complete the following sentence: 'I can (run/jump/draw, etc) very well.'

Opening up

Give each child an unpeeled 'well done' sticker. Choose one child and ask her to unpeel the sticker and put it on someone else's jumper. As they do so, they need to say, *'I am giving you this because you are* (good at being kind, good at helping me, etc)'. When each child has received a sticker, go round the group and ask them to repeat the reason why they were given the smiley face. Did they like to receive the sticker and the kind words from their classmates? They can give other people this warm feeling at any time because all they have to do is smile and say something nice. Now see if they can think of someone who might like to receive the gift of some kind words – their mum or dad perhaps. Set them the task of remembering to say something kind to everyone at home and at school every day and see how much happiness they can make all by themselves.

Cheering up

Smiles are very 'catching' and a very good thing to share. Tell the children the following rhyme – pick up the smiley puppet or show them the picture of a smiley person and say:

Here's smiley Sue.

What shall we do?

Her smile's so bright,

We are smiling too.

Calming down

Play the cheerful music and ask the children to move their arms and legs in a light, floating light way to the rhythm of the music until everyone is in a happy frame of mind.

To help children self-praise, give each of them a red sticky dot. They can put it on any piece of work they have done that they think is good for any reason they can offer. If they are proud of a kind act they did during the week, they do a drawing of it and put a red dot on it. They can bring these to Circle Time to talk about.

MONARCH OF THE REALM

SEAL theme: Good to be me

Focus: To give a boost to everyone's self-esteem and provide children with a sense of personal power

What you need: Speaking object; crown; a cloak; cheerful orchestral music or a rainstick

> Role-playing social interaction provides children with a means of trying out different ways of responding in a safe setting.

Meeting up

Choose a child to be 'it', who then has to leave the room, and another child to be 'chief'. The chief acts out short movements (eg clapping hands three times and stomping feet four times). All other players must do what the chief does. The 'it' person returns to the group to figure out who is the Big Chief. Everyone must concentrate so that they can follow the Big Chief's movements without a pause.

Warming up

Using the speaking object, ask each child in turn to complete the sentence: *'If I met a king, I would say ...'* Children who do not wish to speak may say 'pass' and give the speaking object to the next child.

Opening up

Tell the children a few days before to imagine that they are all 'Monarch of the Realm' and that they can issue any royal decree that they like. This can be as preposterous as they wish: the object is to use their imagination and have fun. For example they might put on the crown and say, *'I am the queen of the realm and I decree that every one of my subjects should wear spotted welly boots in the sunshine.'* The monarch then passes the crown on to the other children so that everyone can have a turn. The last royal personage to pass a decree is then given the task of introducing the Wizard to the Royal Court of Children by choosing someone and giving them the magic cloak. This wizard can make a wish on behalf of the group. This may be a visit to the park or a party or whatever they wish.

> **If you have a child in your class who really needs a boost, you need to either take the crown and choose them yourself or prompt the current monarch to choose that particular child. Under the safety of a crown or a cloak, many shy children find the courage to do things that they would never do in real life!**

Finally, the wizard can lead the children in a game of 'Wizard Says' which is just like 'Simon Says' but much more magical!

Cheering up

Use this little rhyme to thank the royal wizard for coming to your circle meeting:

Wizard (insert child's name) is here today

We'll all clap our hands and say,

'It's good to see you, Wizard.'

Remind the children that they are ALL important, magical and special. Ask everybody to stand up and hold hands. Swing your arms high and chant, *'We are special'* as you do so. Repeat a couple of times.

Calming down

Ask the children to close their eyes and put their hands on knees with the palms facing upwards and their fingers lightly curled. Using a rain-stick or mood music, allow them to think about what makes them special.

I felt scared but excited pretending to be a queen, telling others what to do

Danielle, aged 10

STOP AND THINK

Theme: Relationships

Focus: To teach the children to be assertive

Group size: 10, up to whole class

What you need: Speaking object

Meeting up

The children sit in a circle. Demonstrate actions, for example, 'Simon says, stand on one foot'. If the order is given without the prefix, 'Simon says', the group must NOT imitate the action or follow the order. Players who move when they should stay still must take a turn out and sit out of the game for three commands.

Warming up

Using the speaking object, ask each child in turn to complete the following sentence: *'I don't like it when people say…'*

Opening up

Use your current storybook, a recent event in class, or something in the news to generate a discussion about a tricky situation experienced by a fictional character. (Using a fictional character is essential because your children need to start this discussion in an atmosphere of safety. They need to be reassured that they will not have to describe their own difficult experiences but can think about them from a distance.) Now explain that it is important to keep safe and out of trouble and difficulties, so we need to learn to stop and think when someone asks us to do something. What might happen if we do what someone is asking us to do? 'No' is a very hard word to say but there are some ways to make it easier.

Look as if you mean it

Stand tall, hands on hips, head up, looking straight ahead. Ask for confident volunteers to come up and demonstrate an assertive 'no', or 'no, thank you' to your prompts to do things like mess up a painting or knock over a box of pencils. All the children can then stand up and say 'no' firmly.

Give reasons

Explain why you don't want to do something: *'No, I don't want to get into trouble'* or *'No, because it would make me feel bad'*. Choose scenarios that are relevant to your situation and practice this technique with some more volunteers.

Give the behaviour a name

Stealing, bullying, being unkind, dishonest, breaking the rules are all examples of things we don't want to do. Teach the children to say, *'No, I won't do that because it's cheating/stealing/naughty'* etc. Give more volunteers scenarios to practise this skill.

Change the subject

Take the conversation into a different topic, away from what you are being asked to do. Again, you can role-play using volunteers or ask the whole assembly to 'repeat after you'. Older children may like to learn to ask questions, like: *'Why do you think that is a good thing to do? Why would you want me to do something like that?'* Tell the children that they can always just walk away or walk away and ask an adult to assist them.

Cheering up

Commend the children on how assertive and independent they are becoming. Be specific, especially towards shy or hesitant children and give them precise feedback to reinforce the lesson. For example, *'Sammy, I really liked the way you held your head up and LOOKED as if you meant every word'*. Ask other children if they can commend anyone who is not their best friend for any recent assertive behaviour they've seen at playtime.

50

Calming down

Ask the children to sit very quietly and to shut their eyes. Tell them to slowly touch their elbows to make sure that they are still there. Now ask them to: gently touch their shoulders to make sure that they are still there and haven't got lost; quietly touch their hair; put their hands in their laps and gently wiggle their toes; gently wiggle their fingers. Then ask them to breathe quietly for a moment or two, open their eyes and 'come back' to the room.

When I opened my eyes I thought I was in a different world

Sakira, aged 11

IN MY OPINION...

When you work together as a group to investigate social, emotional and behavioural issues you all need to know when facts are a necessity and when opinions can be expressed.

SEAL theme: Relationships

Focus: To facilitate smooth social interaction

What you need: Speaking object, pictures of animals or a collection of animal toys

Meeting up

The children should crouch down to balance on arms and legs in a large circle, facing towards the centre. Number the children 1, 2, 3 and again 1, 2, 3 and so on around the circle. When a number is called, all of the children with that number can move one limb. The numbers need to be called quite quickly. The object of the activity is to cross the circle without touching anyone else so there needs to be considerable co-operation and manoeuvring. For example, a child may have to move backwards or sideways to allow another child to pass.

Warming up

Using the speaking object, ask each child in turn to complete the following sentence: *'My favourite animal is ...'* Children who do not wish to speak may say 'pass' and give the speaking object to the next child.

Opening up

Point out that a lot of people chose different animals but there were no wrong answers. It was all a question of taste and everyone had their own reasons for making their particular choice. Hold up a toy giraffe and tell the children that you are going to say three things about it:

'This giraffe has four legs.' (a fact)
'It has long legs.' (another fact)
'Giraffes are pretty.' (an opinion)

You can then ask for a show of hands. *'Who agrees that this is a giraffe?'* (It is a fact so everybody should agree.) *'Who agrees that it has four legs?'* (This is also a fact so everyone should put up his or her hand.) *'Who agrees that it is pretty?'* (There should be a variety of opinions here.) Repeat this activity with another animal. Now ask the children to think of another animal and state two facts about it and then add an opinion. Point out that we can hold opinions that are very different. For example, one child may think that lions are cuddly while another may think that they are quite frightening. Ask the children to research the range of opinions about animals.

> You can extend this idea later by showing the children how to research strength of opinion. Give them a prepared survey sheet that gives a range of opinion – hate/dislike/like/like very much – and an issue to research, such as 'Opinions about dogs'.

Now you can show the children how we justify opinions by telling them how we use the word 'because'. It's a word that means 'for the reason that follows'. Put the children into groups of three and give them an animal and a large card with the word 'because' printed on it. Ask each group to think of facts about the animal and to discuss their opinions about it. They can then hold up their picture and describe it using facts, and then share their opinions. For example:

Ist child:	'We like this animal…' (expresses opinion)
2nd child:	'because' (holds up card)
3rd child:	'it has interesting habits and runs very fast.' (our reasons)

You can then develop this by asking them to follow the same format when discussing more abstract issues, such as: 'We don't like noisy people because it is hard to concentrate when they are around.'

Cheering up

Tell the children that you know some facts about them: they are all in your class, they are a group of boys and girls, and so on. Then tell them that you are of the opinion that they are also quite wonderful because……….. . (Prepare a list of positive comments about your class from your teaching assistants, other support staff, school secretary etc.)

Calming down

Ask the children to take three or four slow deep breaths and imagine that they are breathing in happiness and breathing out unhappiness until their whole body feels peaceful and content. Pause for moment and then think of positive words to tell themselves. These can be thought as 'I' statements – 'I am lovely. I am good at many things, I am happy' etc.

ALL CHANGE

SEAL theme: Changes

Focus: Adjusting to change

What you need: Speaking object; a copy of the story of Snow White or any story that is relevant to your classroom activities

Meeting up

Ask children to volunteer or choose a child to begin a movement that is to be copied by the player who is sitting on your right. In turn and without speaking, each person in the circle should perform the action until the action has come full circle. Now change the action and begin the process again.

Warming up

Using the speaking object, ask each child in turn to complete the following sentence: 'If I changed into a story character, I would be...' Children who do not wish to speak may say 'pass' and give the speaking object to the next child.

Opening up

Tell or recap the story of Snow White and make a list of the major changes that take place in her life. Talk about how these changes must have affected every aspect of her daily life. Take contributions from the children. What strategies do they think she might have used to get used to the changes? (Take her time, relax, think about things carefully, try to look on the bright side and so on.) Talk about the changes that might take place in your children's lives: change of class or a new school. Choose one of these and decide which strategies might help. Take suggestions from the children using the sentence stem, 'Would it help if...?'

Cheering up

Change is difficult, however old we are. Congratulate the children on sharing their adjustment strategies and ask them to give themselves a clap. Ask if any child would like to teach the others a new game which may change the games they play at lunchtime. If you are not sure anybody will volunteer on the day then the day before offer your book of games to any child prepared to teach others in the circle. The child then chooses six volunteers to come in the middle so they can teach them a new activity or game. Clapping games are very popular. After they've taught a game and sat down again, the outside circle is encouraged to give feedback on the quality of their teaching. Ask them all to see if they could be brave enough to teach this new skill to younger children in the playground today.

Calming down

Repeat the meeting-up game.

> **TOP TIP**
>
> **Sometimes, you can reuse your meeting-up game as a calming down game to reinforce the skill it teaches.**

USING SEAL GUIDANCE IN QUALITY CIRCLE TIME MEETINGS

The SEAL toolkit offers you a wealth of practical ways to achieve your learning objectives, with a yearly cycle of six themes and an additional short focus on the issue of bullying. A great deal of thought has been invested in the structure of these themes and the DfES would clearly prefer you to use them for the following reason: 'Schools and settings should be aware that within the suggested sequence of themes later work sometimes builds on key concepts taught earlier in the year.'

DfES Guidance for the Primary National Strategy, *Excellence and Enjoyment: social and emotional aspects of learning*, page 18.

But the choice is yours: you can decide to fit the resource into your existing curriculum OR you can choose to fit your existing curricular materials in with the cycle of themes in the SEAL pack. In other words, nobody is asking you to throw away what you already have, but you will be expected to be familiar with what SEAL has to offer and to use the materials in your planning for social and emotional development. The SEAL themes are:

New beginnings   **Good to be me**

Getting on and falling out   **Relationships**

Say no to bullying   **Changes**

Going for goals!

Each primary year group has a booklet of activities that have been produced for each theme. These booklets provide clear descriptions of the intended learning outcomes that are made into positive 'I' statements that will prove useful when you write your own Circle

Time meetings. They can be found in Appendix One of the Guidance document. For example, the statements, *'I know that everybody in the world has feelings'*, *'I like the ways we are all different'* and *'I like belonging to my group/class/school'* can form the core of many successful meetings if you tailor them to the specific needs of your group or class. These affirmations can then be taught to the children, helping them to develop a positive image.

The lesson plans in the SEAL pack often begin with the first two steps used in Quality Circle Time meetings and use the words 'Learning Opportunities' as an alternative to 'Opening Up'. There are many useful suggestions in the SEAL documents to show you the different ways that you can approach this vital stage of your Circle Time meetings.

However, Quality Circle Time meetings always end with two further activities. The first is 'Cheering Up' when success is celebrated (the positive 'I' statements in the SEAL guidance document will come in very useful here!). Finally, a calming game or short reflection completes the meeting. The SEAL document does not always offer advice about how you should bring your meetings to a close but these two steps from the Quality Circle Time model will help you to do so in an appropriate manner.

Each SEAL toolkit offers activities, scripts and interactive stories that are specifically designed to fit their purpose. You are also told exactly how to use them and are provided with examples of suitable questions. You don't need to spend hours searching for stories, scripts, activities and pictures that describe the scenarios you want children to think about – you have them at your fingertips.

The SEAL package is well grounded in excellent primary practice. We at Jenny Mosley Consultancies are proud to have made a contribution. SEAL has brought so much together and presented it in an accessible and straightforward way. We sometimes open packages from the DfES with a sense of unease but SEAL is an outstanding exception: a truly useful and uplifting set of practical suggestions.

HOW TO USE THE SEAL TOOLKIT FOR CIRCLE TIME MEETINGS

An exemplar meeting – although we know 'life' isn't always this straight forward!

Mr Thompson has a Year 3 class of 30 mixed ability children. The school's catchment area means that children come from a wide variety of social backgrounds. They are generally well integrated as a class but Mr Thompson is aware that tensions sometimes surface because a small number of children tend to assume that they have the right to lead group activities and a few of these children use their power in antisocial ways. He has also noticed that other class members feel frustrated and resentful of this perceived domination but don't seem to have learned skills that would help them to resist peer pressure.

Mr Thompson decides that his class would benefit from learning how to be more assertive. He intends to address this need in a Circle Time meeting. Before he begins planning the meeting, he reads through the following collection of SEAL documents:

Good to be me – theme overview
Excellence and Enjoyment – Guidance
Good to be me – staff-room activities
Good to be me – family activities
Good to be me – Years 3 and 4
Good to be me – small group activities

1. From the **theme overview**, he selects the following learning objectives for PSHE/Citizenship:

   3f) Children will be taught that pressure to behave in an unacceptable or risky way can come from a variety of sources, including people they know, and how to ask for help and use basic techniques for resisting pressure to do wrong.

   4a) Children will be taught that their actions affect themselves and others, to care about other people's feelings and to try to see things form their point of view. (page 2)

2. He adds positive 'I' statements to these objectives to clarify what he wants the children to know, understand and be able to do as a result of the Circle Time meetings:

   'I can choose to act assertively.'
   'I know how to be assertive.'
   'I can express myself assertively in a variety of ways.' (page 6)

3. He is aware that these Circle Time meetings may arouse strong feelings so he reads Appendix four in the **Guidance** document to ensure that his approach complies with guidelines. This document reminds him that the class must refocus on their ground rules before each Circle Time meeting.

4. He checks with his head-teacher that the **staff-room activity** concerning assertiveness is scheduled prior to the classroom activities so that he is aware of his own feelings about assertiveness. The head-teacher confirms that assertiveness skills will be studied in every classroom and that all members of staff, particularly lunchtime supervisors are aware that it is being highlighted throughout the school.

5. Mr Thompson then selects, 'Making a worry catcher' from the **Family Activities** booklet as a homework assignment.

6. He then plans the Circle Time meeting to introduce assertiveness.

Step one – Meeting up game
'There's a chair on my right.' (page 22)

Step two – Warming up round
Mr Thompson thinks of a suitable round to fit in with the above game. 'I know someone is a friend when he/she …
(helps me/is kind/plays with me etc)."

Step three – Opening up
He selects the 'being assertive' activity. (page 8)

Step four – Cheering up
Mr Thompson has been keeping a note of children who are pro-socially assertive. At this point he recounts details of times when they have used their assertiveness skills and asks everyone to give them a clap. He asks all the children to keep track of other children (not their best friends) who, during the week, use some of the assertive skills they've just learnt. Next week they can be nominated and voted for by the class and, later, receive certificates signed by everyone in the class.

Step five – Calming down
He uses the visualisation exercise, 'Melting in the Sun'* in the **small group activities booklet**.

*Children love ritual – it's OK if you use activities from other 'sets' sometimes.

Part Three: Designing Your Own Quality Circle Times

Now you are ready to plan Circle Time meetings that are uniquely suited to your children's particular needs. The following pages will give you the information you need to plan really successful sessions, but we will begin with a list of points that you need to bear in mind when you do your planning.

THE SKILLS OF CIRCLE TIME

Be constructive

When you lead a Circle Time meeting, your objective is to build emotionally strong, resilient children who are confident in their ability to achieve and be successful. Put-downs and ridicule destroy trust, and cause vulnerable children to become defensive and unresponsive. It is vital that you use Circle Time to teach, model, praise and reinforce the values and behaviour that will give each child positive ways of learning and interacting.

Be clear about your objectives

Your planning needs to be driven by learning outcomes: the teaching of social, emotional and behavioural skills and universal moral values. Keep this in mind when you plan your sessions. Meetings that are purely activity-driven may be fun, but they are less likely to successfully change behaviour and raise self-esteem. Similarly, it is a good idea to try to keep things simple and straightforward. It is much better to investigate one aspect of an issue carefully and thoroughly than to try and cover too much at once.

Circle Time meetings need to be well-paced and it is important that children don't become bored. Never let them have too much of a favourite activity. Save some of its excitement for the next session and the one after that. Then you will have a class that looks forward to Circle Time with eager anticipation.

Use a wide variety of approaches

The list of teaching and learning techniques that can be used in circle time is long and varied. Don't be afraid to try new things. Adapt techniques from PE, mathematics and other lessons. Keep an open mind and you will soon find that all of these techniques can be used to teach social, emotional and behavioural skills.

Keep it emotionally safe

We all have times when talking about personal and emotional issues can seem threatening. However, these dangers can be sidestepped by taking children into the safety of story-world. If you use puppets, poems, drama and stories, you can discuss emotional problems through imaginary characters because they allow children to think about tricky issues without having to refer to 'real' life events. The issues remain the same, the characters' responses and behaviour are entirely human, but somehow the imaginary context takes away the vulnerability and creates a place of safety in each child's mind.

Plan carefully but be flexible

You need to have a clear well-structured plan ready before each session so that you know how you intend to get from A to B. You also need to be prepared to accommodate the unexpected. Much of the curriculum is closely controlled, but Circle Time is one occasion when you need to be open to the possibility of being 'child led' and adaptable.

Be child-centred

Though one of your objectives will be to extend each child's range of 'feeling' words, it is important that you make difficult, complex subjects easier by talking and demonstrating in ways that they will understand. Circle Time is democratic, so give your children every opportunity to explain to you in their own words and praise them for their efforts. Remember that your children are looking to you for guidance. Model the behaviours that you wish to promote – listen carefully, maintain good eye contact, be warm and reflect back to show that you understand what the children are saying.

Review frequently

It is vital that your Circle Time meetings don't become stale or routine. Review how they are going and seek ways to re-energise them if you feel that the children are losing interest. The subjects you are exploring during Circle Time meetings are important to us all so should never seem boring. Always adapt plans to suit the very particular needs of your class and environment.

The 'round' is a great 'review' tool for feedback on everything! The day before, tell the children you'll be having a round of 'one thing I'd like to change about Circle Time'. Or if, as a school, you want to review the quality of lunchtimes, you could have a round from the children; 'would it help...'. In Step 3 they could then debate the validity of the ideas.

WRITING YOUR OWN PLANS

The issue

Begin by choosing the issue you wish to work on. This will be the subject of the 'opening up' phase of the meeting. You **must** start your planning in this way by deciding on the content of the **middle section** of the meeting.

The strategy

Decide which teaching strategy is best suited to the way you want to approach the issue. These are explained in detail on the following pages. You can choose issues that are generated by the curriculum or situations that are specific to your particular class or group. Don't forget it is a good idea to have a Circle Time suggestion box in your classroom. Any child can put in anonymous notes. I once found one that said, 'What do you do, cos you can't sleep at night, cos you haven't got a best friend'. Through puppets we then explored the issue of 'Kindness and Friendship'.

Putting it all together

Once you have chosen a theme for your circle meeting, you will be ready to select appropriate activities for each of the five steps. Each step has a different purpose but you need to make sure that the meeting flows from one activity to the next in a way that makes sense to all the participants. Each step adds something to your chosen theme. Don't choose games and visualisations that have nothing to do with the subject you have chosen to investigate in the 'opening up' phase of the meeting.

We will now look at each step in more detail.

STEP ONE

MEETING UP

Playing a game

Each meeting begins with a game. The purpose of the game is to:

- *warm everybody up*
- *help children relax*
- *bring the children together as a group*
- *ensure children feel the idea that being part of the group is fun*
- *build group identity*
- *practise the skills of concentrating, listening, taking turns, etc*
- *take their minds off all their worries and problems*

MEETING UP GAMES

Fruit basket

This game is designed to mix the children so that they are not sitting with their friends

The children sit in a circle. Go around the group and label each child either an orange or lemon. Now call out 'oranges', or 'lemons' or 'fruit basket'. The children in the named category must change places. When fruit basket is called, everybody changes places. The categories of this game can be changed to fit with your theme. You could use colours, football teams, animals – the range is limitless!

The magic box

... helps develop attentive looking skills

Place an imaginary box in the centre of the circle. A child goes to the 'box' and 'takes out' something and demonstrates its use. The other children guess what it is: hairbrush, golf club, snooker cue etc. Everyone copies the mime and the next child in the circle has a turn to demonstrate and so on around the circle.

Car chase

The children sit in a circle and someone starts the 'car' going around the circle by saying 'zoom' and turning his head quickly to the person to the right. That player repeats the word, 'zoom' and the action – the 'car' 'zooms' around the circle until someone says, 'Eek!' which means the 'car' changes direction and the 'zoom' sound goes in the other direction until the next 'eek!'.

...develops concentration skills

Simon says

The children call out and demonstrate actions, such as 'Simon says, stand on one foot.' If the order is given without the prefix, 'Simon says', the group must NOT imitate the action or follow the order. Players who move when they should stay still must sit out of the game for three commands.

...develops concentration skills

Ready for action

Show the children a selection of actions that correspond with visual cues. For example:

...concentration and quick thinking are learned when you play this game

When the leader touches his elbow, the children jump up and down.

When the leader raises her arm, the children hop on the spot.

When the leader folds his arms, the children lie down.

The children must react correctly to the visual cues and watch carefully to see the next cue so that they can change action immediately. When everyone is familiar with the game you can ask children to make up their own cues and lead the game.

Who's talking now

The children sit in a circle and you have to choose one to be the monarch. This child stands in the centre of the circle wearing the blindfold. On the command, 'Go' the other children walk round the circle until the monarch calls, 'Stop'. She then points straight ahead and asks, *'Who goes there, friend or foe?'* The child who is being pointed at answers, *'Why, friend of course your Majesty.'* The monarch should now try to guess the identity of the speaker. If they guess correctly, the two of them swap places. If the guess is incorrect, the monarch stays in the centre and a new game begins.

Clap this way

Form the circle and explain to the children that they are going to clap some rhythms. At the same time you are going to call out instructions that they must follow. For example:

Clap high (clap above your head) 1, 2, 3, 4

Clap low (clap down by your knees) 1, 2, 3, 4

Clap to the right, 1, 2, 3, 4

Clap to the left, 1, 2, 3, 4

Clap with your partner (both hands together) 1, 2, 3, 4

Follow the leader

The leader begins with a movement that is copied by the player who is sitting on her right. In turn and without speaking, the action is performed by each person in the circle until the action has come full circle. The leader then changes the action and the process begins again.

Tangles

The children stand in a circle, close their eyes and walk slowly towards the centre. With eyes still closed they each find two other hands to hold. The children then open their eyes and have to try to untangle themselves without letting go of hands, until they can all stand in an inward facing circle.

...builds trust

Wink murder

The children sit in a circle. Choose a child to be the detective, who must then leave the room. Choose another child to be the wink murderer. The detective can then return to move slowly around in the centre of the circle. Without being seen by the detective, the murderer winks at any child who then sits down. This continues until the detective correctly identifies the murderer. Continue with different children in the roles.

...improves observation skills

Change the action

Explain that the children are all going to make the same hand movements. Once all the children are doing this, the leader walks behind the chairs and taps someone on the back. That person counts to five in their head and then changes the movement. Once all the children are doing the new movement, the leader touches another child on the back. It is a good idea to show the children some simple hand movements first to give a general idea of what to do.

...improves attention skills

The orchestra

Divide the children into small groups around the circle. Each group must decide on a sound, eg *boom-boom, ta-te-te-ta, rrrrr, ticka, ticka, ticka.* Explain that the children are musicians in an orchestra

...helps listening skills

and you are going to be the conductor. Demonstrate the gestures that will be used:

Pointing to different groups to join in

Making a halt sign for groups to stop

Finger on lips for quietly

Raising both hands for loudly

Using hands for tempo

Pulling hands apart for 'all stop'

Continue until the children are ready for the next activity.

Trust

...helps children to concentrate and gets their 'thinking brain' working

Choose one child from the circle to stand blindfolded in the centre. Pass an object such as a ruler or book around the circle until the child in the centre calls, 'Stop'. Everyone else should now give the child verbal directions to locate the object, eg turn left, move six paces forward, move slightly to your right, two paces forward and so on. Choose another child and begin the game again.

Crossing the circle

...helps self control and listening

The children should crouch down to balance on arms and legs in a large circle, facing towards the centre. Number the children 1, 2, 3 and again 1, 2, 3 and so on around the circle. When a number is called, all of the children with that number can move one limb. The numbers need to be called quite quickly. The object of the activity is to cross the circle without touching anyone else so there needs to be considerable co-operation and manoeuvring. For example, a child may have to move backwards or sideways to allow another child to pass.

Express yourself

Ask the children to cover their faces with their hands. Now name different facial expressions to indicate emotions: smiling, frowning, anger, laughter, crying. At each one the children should silently mime the look, and remove their hands to reveal the appropriate expression. To close, the group can pass a smile around the group.

...helps children to read faces

On cue

Name a cue word and explain that when everyone hears this word they must perform an action, for example, *'I'm going to talk about the weather. Every time you hear the word "rain" put your hands on your head.'* Now make up a story and use the cue word frequently.

...supports excellent listening

Changing seats

Call a child's name – this child must then changes places with you. The same child then calls the name of another child, changes places and sits down. This continues until all the children are seated.

...moves people round

Pass a smile

Smile at the child on your right, who should then pass the smile around the circle.

...encourages eye contact.

I know your name

One child must call another's name and roll a ball to them. The recipient then calls out another child's name and repeats the action. The game continues until all the children have had a turn. Children should fold their arms when they have had a turn.

...getting to know you

Name clap

Each child in the circle should say their name in turn. As they say the name, they must clap its rhythm by syllable.

...everyone is noticed

Listen and touch

Tell the children to touch something with their thumb, little finger, elbow, knee etc. For example, 'Touch the floor with your elbow. Touch your teeth with your little finger. Touch your nose with your thumb.' Continue until everyone is attentive and ready for the next activity.

...helps listening and co-ordination

Finger rhyme

Worms live in a hole (wiggle fingers downwards)

A bird lives in a tree (flutter fingers upwards)

Fish live in the river (wiggle fingers horizontally)

But home is the place for me! (point to self)

...releases tension in hands

First and last names

Using the initial of their first and surnames, the children have to respond to the questions that you ask, around the circle. For example, *'John Brown, what is your special food?'* John could answer, *'Juicy bangers'*, *'Jumpy beetroot,'* or *'Jelly beans'* and so on. (Make sure you have a selection of questions ready: holiday destination, hobby, game etc.)

...helps them to enjoy words. Tip – give them time before circle time to work out answers

Things we have in common

Call out different categories: anyone with a November birthday, anyone who likes maths, anyone who swims for a hobby, etc. Children who feel that they fit with the named category must go to the centre of the circle and greet the others.

...helps children find 'bonds'

I went to...

One child begins a sentence such as 'I went to the zoo and saw an elephant'. The next child repeats and adds another animal: 'I went to the zoo and saw an elephant and a tiger'. This continues around the circle with each child repeating the previous sentence and adding another animal. When someone makes a mistake or cannot think of a new animal, they are allowed to begin a new sentence.

...really helps memory skills

Word associations

Name a word of your choice. The child next to you must say the word that she associates with your word. Everyone should join in with two claps to separate the words. A round might go like this: rain (clap clap), cold (clap clap), handkerchief (clap, clap), white (clap, clap). If anyone falters, or cannot think of a word, they begin a new sentence. See how fast the participants can get this game going around the circle.

...whole-brain workouts

Gloop

Throw some imaginary slime over the child sitting next to you. The imaginary slime should be passed from one pupil to the next. The 'slime' must always land on the person's face and as it is pulled off, the group can make slurping noises. This game is a great energiser if the mood in the group is a bit flat.

...generates good eye contact and much laughter – but can hype some classes up too much

Pass the snake

Tell the children that they are now going to mime passing objects around the circle from one person to the next. Choose one player to mime passing a snake in an appropriate manner. After the snake has been passed several times change the object and continue the game. Examples of objects might be a hot plate of soup, a heavy suitcase, a sticky bun, a foul-smelling experiment.

...drama and mime are always fun

Pass the beanbag

...really helps children to work together

Put the children into two teams by naming them red, yellow, red, yellow, red etc. Give someone in each team a beanbag – they should be on opposite sides of the circle. At a signal, the beanbags are passed in the same direction from person to person belonging to the same team. The purpose is to see if one team can move its beanbag from player to player at such a speed that it overtakes the ball from the opposing team. If this happens one point is scored and the game begins again. The first team to score three points wins. Remember that the beanbag must be relayed between players of each team without hindering the opposing team.

Big chief

...helps boost self esteem of shy children

Choose a child to be 'it', who then has to leave the room. Another child is chosen to be chief. The chief acts out short movements, clapping hands three times, stomping feet four times, for example. All other players must do what the chief does. The 'it' person returns to the group to figure out who is the Big Chief, so everyone must concentrate so that they can follow the Big Chief's movements without a pause.

Ha ha ha

...breaks tension; helps laughter

One child has to look at the person on her right and say 'Ha' as seriously as possible. The next player must say 'Ha ha', and so on, each child adding an extra 'ha' each time. Anyone who laughs has to stand outside the circle and can pull funny faces (without touching any of the players) to try to make the other children laugh.

Floors

...helps miming skills. You could choose just one or two to go inside circle – others guess

Make a circle with sufficient space for the children to move around inside. Explain to the children that they are going to walk around pretending they are on different surfaces. Start with thick, squelchy mud. At intervals, change the surface: slippery ice, a trampoline, quicksand, hot coals, glue.

STEP TWO

WARMING UP

Breaking the silence

This step focuses on a 'round' to help children to feel confident about speaking up. The leader begins a simple sentence which is completed by the child on the leader's right. Each child speaks in turn until everyone has had a go. A 'speaking object' is used to show whose turn it is to speak. Whoever is holding the speaking object has the right to speak without being interrupted. Once they have spoken, each child passes the speaking object on to the person on their right. The speaking object needs to be small enough to fit into a child's hand – a painted egg works very well but many leaders choose a small fluffy toy or 'talking teddy'. Alternatively, you may like to use an object that is linked to your current themes in class. The purpose of 'Warming up' is to:

> *Remind children that they all have the right to speak*
>
> *Remind children that they all have the responsibility to listen attentively*
>
> *Practise turn-taking*
>
> *Help focus on the theme of the meeting*

Points to remember:

- Make sure that the round is relevant to the theme of the meeting.

- Any child who does not wish to speak can say 'pass' and hand the speaking object to the child on their right.

- If you notice that many children are opting out of this step by saying 'pass', you can give them a chance to think about what they will say by telling them the beginning of the sentence before the meeting. You might even tell them the day before and explain that you want them to think about what they will say. Some children may prefer to write their contribution on a piece of card or practise it with you before the meeting. Alternatively, you can use a puppet to chat to the children about what will happen in the meeting. The puppet might offer to speak for any child who feels shy. The child can then tell the puppet their sentence before the meeting and the puppet will say it at the appropriate time.

The following sentence starters work well as rounds:

ROUNDS FOR THE 'WARMING UP' STEP

Self-awareness/empathy

I feel happy when I hear…
I feel happy when I see…
I feel happy when I smell…
I feel happy when I touch…
I feel happy when I taste…
One thing that really annoys me is…
I like it when…
I think the world would be better if…
I feel lonely when…
I feel safe when…
I feel scared when…
The most scary place in school is…
I like to be noisy/quiet when…
Silence makes me feel…
I like to be alone when…
My favourite animal is…
If I changed into an animal, I would be…

Sometimes, I regret…
The last time I was really embarrassed was when…
I know my friend is unhappy when…
I can make my friends happy by…
Something I like about myself is…
When it is wet and rainy, I like…
My favourite story is…

Social skills

I like it when my friends…
I don't like it when my friends…
When I say sorry, I feel…
I feel threatened when…
I really appreciate it when…
I don't want people to call me…
I don't like it when people say…
When someone helps me, I feel…
I like to play with… because…
I say 'thank you' when…
The best thing we can do to celebrate is…
I would say 'no' if…
To make people happy, I can…
I know… is my friend because…
I make other people cross when I…
I made the right choice when I…
If I met a king, I would say…
If I had a prize, I would give it to…

Motivation

One thing I am looking forward to is…
When I make a mistake, I feel…
If I ruled the world, I would…
My ambition is…
One target I want to achieve today is…

The most frustrating thing for me is...
The person I admire most is... because...
When I was small...
If I could not fail, I would...
I relax by...
Something interesting that I learned recently is...
Sometimes, I worry about...
I can do... very well...

STEP THREE

OPENING UP

Exploring issues that concern the class

This is the most challenging phase of any circle meeting. We call it 'Open Forum' because it offers everyone an opportunity to explore important issues. Its structure allows the leader to use a wide variety of teaching strategies. The children's concerns can be approached in ways that capture attention while being investigated in an environment of emotional safety.

The purpose of 'Opening Up' is to:
- Teach children productive ways to express their opinions
- Develop reasoning skills and logical thinking
- Value diversity and appreciate the need for open mindedness
- Learn the skills of constructive discussion
- Promote self- and group-esteem through the acknowledgment that every child has the ability to make healthy decisions and responsible choices
- Allow children to rehearse life-skills and problem-solving techniques in a safe environment
- Support cooperative target-setting for individuals and the group

Points to remember

- Keep it simple – it is better to cut complex issues into bite-sized chunks.
- Keep it safe. Make ground rules clear before each session so that everyone knows the boundaries of the discussion. You may decide to concentrate on in-school matters during some meetings and,

therefore, need to ensure that all children are aware of this ground rule before the 'Opening up' phase of the meeting begins

- Use metaphors or analogies to help children to discuss difficult issues. These create a sense of safety because they can be used to explore problems, concerns, hopes and fears in the safety of imaginary worlds and situations and do not require children to share their personal realities. Analogical tools include stories, puppets, role play, drama and dressing up.

TEACHING/LEARNING STRATEGIES FOR 'OPENING UP'

Peer support through simple scripts

Peer helping contributes to a climate of care and respect in your classroom community. Children often want to help one another but do not always know how or what to do. Children do not make decisions for their classmates but learn how to suggest options and alternatives and share their own experiences. The leader asks if there is anyone who needs help and invites children to raise their hand and state simply, *'I need help because I........'* They may request help with emotional or social problems or may state that they are worried about the curriculum, community issues, understanding what is going on in the world at large etc. Their peers can respond by saying, *'Would it help if I/we/you............'* The needy child thinks about the suggestions he/she has been offered and thanks everyone for their assistance. It is then possible for the group and the child to make an action plan which the child puts into action. The effectiveness of this plan is reviewed during the next Circle Time meeting and the action plan can be refined. Only one child at a time can be helped in this way so you need share out this 'sharing time' fairly through the year. Adults can ask for help too. The best resource in a school is children's minds.

Discussion

Discussions help people with different points of view to learn from each other and search for agreement or compromise. A successful discussion enables children to share what they know and believe and find connections with one another. For this to happen, the theme of the discussion needs to be something to which everyone can relate. Topics that produce fruitful discussion need to reflect the real, lived experience of your group and their hopes, aspirations and fears. Use Circle Time as an opportunity to explain and demonstrate the behaviours that ensure that discussions are productive and positive. These include: taking turns, sensitive listening, appropriate use of vocabulary and facial expression. Explain the different roles in a discussion – observer, questioner, leader, speaker, listener – and demonstrate that all of these roles are valued and praised. Agree ground rules:

- We agree that one speaker at a time should speak

- We listen carefully to one another

- We agree that different viewpoints should be heard

- We always look for agreement and compromise

- We always look for solutions

After a topic has been introduced you can begin a discussion with a question like, *'Who would like to agree with ....?'* or with a statement like, *'There are a lot of different opinions about .... Some people agree with this idea but other people have strong arguments against it. Let's look at all the different points of view.'* After listening to a range of points of view, you need to model how to sum up and find points of consensus.

Drama

Drama gives children the opportunity to use their imagination to investigate a wide range of real issues that may cause fear or distress. Dramatic activity can be approached in a wide variety of ways:

- **Mime** – The group represents actions, character or mood using only gestures and movements rather than words. This enables children to learn to 'read' body language. Background sound effects can be used to create a heightened sense of drama.

- **Role play** – Role play aims to bring situations and events to life and enables children to 'experience' what it means to be another person or how it feels to be in an unfamiliar situation. This helps them to develop a more sensitive understanding of a variety of viewpoints. They draw on their own experiences but are guided to improvise and think laterally. Role play can be used to illustrate important issues or dilemmas like different ways to deal with bullying or peer pressure. It can be used to teach pro-social behaviours such as how to respond to praise or criticism. Situations that cause anxiety, like visiting the dentist, can be made safer by acting them out in the imaginary arena of a role play. Children can travel into the past, future or to distant locations and examine social, moral issue or situations that cause anxiety. When role-play is used in a Circle Time meeting, it has the added advantage of allowing children to witness how a behaviour looks when it is being 'modelled' by their peers.

- **Action replay** – A short play is devised and shown. It is then replayed with audience participation. The group of observers are allowed to call out, 'Stop', replace a character and show how they could change the situation and move towards a different ending. For instance, a group may show a play about peer pressure and the audience can be invited to 'stop' the replay and demonstrate refusal skills.

- **Doubling** – This works in a similar way to 'action replay' but does not involve enacting the role-play twice. During an enactment, members of the audience are encouraged to leave their seats, stand beside a character and put a hand on his/her shoulder. They then speak to the 'character' and offer a contribution to their situation. This may involve advice like, *'Would it help if ……?'* or an empathetic response like, *'I feel so sorry that you have this problem'* or, *'I'm so pleased that you are feeling happier.'* This strategy ensures the active involvement of the whole group and deepens their empathy.

- **Thought tunnel** – In this activity, children stand in two rows, facing one another. A dilemma or situation is described or enacted by a third group who then walk between the lines. Each person in the line then offers advice. When the group reach the end of the line they are required to make a decision and enact the outcome of the situation.

- **Hot seating** – The teacher or a child must get 'inside' a character as completely as possible. The group then questions the character about their behaviour, motivation and background. Characters can be hot-seated individually, in pairs or in groups. This technique has the added benefit of developing the group's questioning skills.

- **Before and after** – The group is asked to invent scenes or incidents that take place years, days, minutes or even seconds before or after a dramatic event. This enables children to concentrate on causes, motivation and consequences. It is particularly useful when you wish to investigate violent or dangerous situations. For instance, you can ask the group to show the events that took place before a fight or to portray the after effects of a robbery without needing to enact the actual events. This ensures that children concentrate on thoughts and responses and do not become overexcited or fretful.

- **Thought tapping** – In this activity, a play can be stopped at any moment with the call to 'freeze'. Each character is then asked to tell the group their thoughts and feelings. This can be done by tapping each one on the shoulder or holding a 'speak' card above their heads. This technique develops the group's empathy and awareness of diversity.

Poetry

Poets have a special way of using words that utilises the power of rhythm and rhyme. Like songs, they can be repeated without losing any of their power and these qualities make them attractive to children. Well-written poems go to the heart of our emotions and spotlight a feeling with shining accuracy. Even a simple nursery rhyme can be used as the starting point for a thought provoking discussion. For instance, the little rhyme, 'Billy and Me' could be shared with a group who need to discuss differences between people.

> One, two three,
>
> I love coffee,
>
> And Billy loves tea,
>
> How different we be,
>
> One, two three,
>
> I love coffee,
>
> And Billy loves tea.

Make a collection of suitable poems and you will be able to use them as starting points for many Circle Time meeting scripts.

Puppets

There are many advantages to using puppets during Circle Time. Children love them because they have a habit of thinking aloud and like to give a running commentary about their inner lives which teaches children a lot about intentions and emotions. Puppets also react in an exaggerated, immediate and visual way that makes their inner world easy to understand. They are also able to close the distance between you and the children with whom you are working.

Once you have a puppet sitting on your lap, you can cross the generation gap and speak as a child.

Puppets are particularly useful when you wish to model and talk about emotions like fear or embarrassment that humans learn to hide. They like to show these feelings and ask children for advice about how to solve their problems. This helps children to share essential problem solving skills and gives them confidence in their ability to think things through. Positive Press have two great books on using puppets – see the end of this book for contact details.

Stories

Many children find it easier to discuss the problems confronted by characters than to talk about their own. Many stories describe the consequences of actions which makes them an ideal vehicle for discussing motivation and overcoming obstacles.

Thinking skills

Explicit articulation of how they think helps children to improve their cognitive processes. Teaching, modelling and practising specific thinking skills like logical thought or problem-solving helps them to function emotionally and socially. You can use sentence stems to help children develop their thinking skills during Circle Time meetings. Like this:

When we compare..., we notice that they are the same in some ways and different in others. This is what we have noticed...

We noticed that the problem built up in a number of stages. These stages were...

I can explain what happened...

I have evidence to explain...

I know this because...

The reason why I came to this conclusion is...

It is a good/bad thing because...

I have looked at the information and I think...

STEP FOUR

CHEERING UP

Celebrating the positive

When you have been investigating difficult issues, it is vital that the meeting is brought slowly to a close in an atmosphere of safety and optimism. The 'Cheering up' phase is used to celebrate individual and group success. This may be immediate praise for the work the children have done in the meeting or a more general celebration of recent personal achievements. The purpose of this step is to:

- Make everyone feel competent, happy and positive.
- Ensure closure when challenging issues have been investigated.
- Provide space for adults and children to give encouraging information to each other.
- Recognise and reward positive behaviour change.
- Remind children of their individual and group targets and celebrate their attainment.
- Remind children they have talents and skills that can cheer each other up.

Points to remember

- Keep a record of examples of positive behaviour. Many leaders keep a notebook in their pocket during the week so that they can record things they notice and celebrate them during this phase of the circle meeting.

- Be specific. Children need precise information about the behaviours you value if they are to repeat them and integrate them into their day-to-day lives.

- Empower the group by inviting children to nominate each other for praise, certificates or a joyful clap. Sometimes it helps to give children a 'script'. *'Who are you pleased with in this class because they never shout out ... so they always create a calm atmosphere?'* and *'Who are you pleased with because they never get into a fight at lunchtime but always show self-control?'* The list is endless – it is up to you to make sure everyone can see something positive about each person in their class!

- Ask individual children to go into the middle of the circle and teach others a game

We are special

Ask the children to stand up. Tell them to swing their arms on each word and chant, 'We are special'. On the word 'special' everyone should raise their arms above their heads; then lower their arms and repeat the sentence and action again.

Devise celebratory chants, songs and rhymes with the children to give a sense of class identity.

STEP FIVE

CALMING DOWN

Bridging children forward

The calming phase of each meeting ensures that children leave the session feeling refreshed and positive. This closing ritual enables everyone to make a smooth transition to the next part of the day. You can play a simple game like passing a tambourine round the group without making a sound or you could lead the group through a guided visualisation. Alternatively, the children can be asked to sit quietly and listen to music or a rain-stick.

> **The purpose of 'Calming down' is to:**
> - Provide an appropriate transitional activity.
> - Touch the children's imagination and allow them to be reminded of their own inner power and strength.
> - Ensure closure so that 'hot' feelings are cooled.

Points to remember

- Take your time – it is important that you do not rush this phase.
- Speak softly and pause frequently if you are speaking or leading a guided visualisation – the children need time to absorb what you are saying.
- Be positive – the children need to leave the meeting feeling confident and peaceful.

ACTIVITIES FOR USE IN THE 'CALMING DOWN' STAGE

Send a ripple

Explain that you are the rain, denoted by waving fingers. Each child must pass the action on around the circle. Now become the thunder and mime this by slapping your knees. Again, the action should be passed around the circle. Finally, 'bring out the sun' by folding your arms and make sure this action is also passed around the circle.

Pass the squeeze

Ask everyone in the circle to join hands and close their eyes. Gently squeeze the hand of the child on your left, who then gently squeezes the hand of the child on his left and so on until the 'squeeze' has passed around the circle and back to the leader.

A calm place

Tell the children that you are going to show them how to calm down when the going gets tough. Explain that we can calm ourselves down by concentrating on our breathing. Show them what you mean by sitting still, and quiet, and letting your breath become steady and slow. Ask them to try this out. Sit quietly for a few minutes before softly telling them what the next activity will be.

Breathing deeply

Tell the children to take a deep breath while you count to three. Then, as you count back to one, ask them to breathe out slowly.

Quiet reflection

Ask the children to sit with straight backs, hands resting gently in their laps. Tell them to close their eyes and to think about their breathing. Tell them that you want them to breathe in a feeling of happiness and, as they breathe out, you want them to breathe out any feelings or thoughts that may be making them unhappy. Next, ask them to think about themselves enjoying a lovely warm summer day, doing things that they really enjoy. Finally, they can open their eyes and become aware of the room and the present moment.

Creative visualisation

A guided visualisation is a journey into the imagination that shows children how to access the places in their mind that offer a feeling of peace and quiet. Speak slowly in a calm, flat voice and leave spaces for the imagination to picture the scenes that are described.

Sit quietly with eyes closed and hands in laps. Read the following script slowly, leaving pauses where the dotted lines appear.

You are going to imagine that you are riding on a magic carpet which will take you to exciting, interesting places. Think of yourself lying on the carpet. What is it like? Imagine the colours, patterns and texture of your carpet...
(Pause)
It lifts up into the air. You feel the wind on your face as the carpet glides through the sky. Below you is the sea twinkling and glistening in the sunlight. You can see things on the water...
(Pause)
Now the carpet is soaring higher as you approach mountains. Look down and see the snow-covered peaks, crisp and white. Feel the cold air – it makes you shiver...
(Pause)
You see a group of skiers on a snowy slope. Imagine them sliding smoothly down, twisting this way and that. You can hear the swish of their skis as they move...
You are past the mountains now and the carpet drops down lower. You feel the air getting warmer and enjoy the sun on your back...
(Pause)
It is now time to travel home. You lie on your back and feel the

gentle swaying of the carpet, thinking of all the things you have seen on your journey.

Try and think of, and write up, lots more visualisations. Children love them.

Coming 'back' after a visualisation

Ask the children to sit very quietly and to shut their eyes. Tell them to slowly touch their elbows to make sure that they are still there! Ask them to: gently touch their shoulders to make sure that they are still there; quietly touch their hair; put their hands in their laps and gently wiggle their toes; gently wiggle their fingers. Then ask them to breathe quietly for a moment or two, stretch, open their eyes and 'come back' to the room.

PUTTING IT ALL INTO PRACTICE

The meeting that follows is designed to show the planning process in practice.

SCENARIO

Miss Green has an uneasy feeling that at least one child in her class is being bullied. Stacey used to be a cheerful little girl who found quite a lot of the work challenging but was always willing to have a go. Now she sits by herself and is often tearful. Her mum says that nothing has happened at home but that Stacey keeps saying that she has a stomach-ache and often asks if she can stay home from school. Miss Green has asked Stacey if anything is worrying her but Stacey just won't talk. Miss Green has asked a few other children if they know what the matter might be but they are quiet on the subject too.

This is how Miss Green goes about planning a circle meeting to investigate this scenario.

Miss Green decides that the 'Opening up' phase of the meeting will be used as a forum to discuss bullying and she will see how the children respond. Because the children in her class have been unwilling to discuss the subject, she decides to approach it from the safety of storybook characters so that no-one, especially Stacey, will feel threatened.

Because the class is currently following a geography topic about European countries, Miss Green decides that she will use the story of Cinderella because she can link it to the Brothers Grimm and

Scandinavia. Drama and role-play will be used to tell the story and she will develop her children's empathy skills by using the 'freeze-stop' technique. This means that she can call 'freeze' at any point during the action and ask the rest of the group to suggest how they think each character must be feeling.

Miss Green will then develop the children's problem-solving skills by asking them to give Cinderella advice. She decides to scaffold this by giving the children the beginning of a sentence and asking them to complete it. The starter is *'Would it help if...?'* If the atmosphere feels right, she will gently guide them towards a discussion of bullying at school.

With the 'Opening up' stage planned, Miss Green looks for relevant ways to open and close the meeting. She chooses a 'Meeting up' game that mixes the children up so that they are not all sitting next to their friends. The round is chosen to get them thinking along the right lines for the bullying theme – in this case, empathy with others – with a prompt sentence such as *'Sometimes I feel left out when...'.* Then she will choose a way to celebrate the positive things that happen during the meeting. To close the session and make sure that everyone leaves the meeting feeling calm and refreshed, Miss Green writes creative visualisation. With all this worked out, the session plan looks like this:

Focus

Understanding how our actions affect other people.

Group size

Whole class

What you need

Speaking object; story of Cinderella; flip chart

Meeting up

Game: 'Fruit basket' (see page 66)

Warming up

The sentence prompt will be 'I feel safe when...'

Opening up

- Read/recap the story of Cinderella.
- Talk about the characters.
- Put the children into small groups. Explain that one child must be Cinderella (or Sidney – the same character but a boy!) The other members will be Ugly Sisters or Ugly Brothers. Ask each group to devise a short scene that shows the Ugly Sisters/Brothers being mean to Cinderella/Sidney.
- Ask volunteers to share their plays with the others. When the play is frozen, take a note of the children's opinions about how each character is feeling, and list key words on the flip chart.
- Choose a confident child to sit in the middle of the circle, to take the role of Cinderella/Sidney. Encourage the group to ask questions to find out how she feels about her situation.
- Ask the children to offer advice that might help Cinderella/Sidney, using the sentence starter *'Would it help if...?'* Record advice on the flip chart. (If the children seem responsive, ask if they know of any situations in real life where a child might feel the way Cinderella/Sidney does.) What could they do to help a child who is feeling this way?

Cheering up

Thank the children for their insight and empathy. Mention any incidents of caring behaviour noticed recently. Teach the children the affirmation: 'I can understand another person's point of view and understand how they might be feeling.'

Calming down

Ask children to sit still and close their eyes. Use the following visualisation:

You walk into a lovely garden.

You feel the sun on your body and a warm breeze ruffles your hair.

You feel the tickle of grass under your bare feet.

You see a gate at the end of the lawn and you walk towards it.

You open the gate and walk through.

You see a lovely picnic party going on.

There are lots of children there. They have kind, smiling faces.

You walk over to join them. They are friendly and welcome you to the party.

You feel safe and happy.

You join in some games. You enjoy yourself.

Now it is time to come back.

Sit very quietly and let your imagination bring you back to the classroom.

When you are ready, open your eyes and smile at the people who are sitting next to you.

What Teachers Ask

What makes a good Circle Time leader?

You need to be proactive and model the behaviours that you wish to instil in your children. Make sure that you have a range of positive rewards ready before each meeting. Be ready to give praise, and more praise, and make sure that you have a list of specific acts and behaviours that you can celebrate during the meeting. No opportunity to give positive feedback should be missed. It's easy during a busy week to forget that you noticed some small achievement so keep a notebook in your pocket for jotting down things you have noticed. Don't neglect the children who are always good. Many teachers find that keeping a little register of praise given ensures that it is distributed fairly.

Does Circle Time suit every child?

The majority of children adapt to Circle Time quickly and look forward to it with enthusiasm, but some find it rigorous and difficult at first. Shy, reticent children may find it hard to express their opinions and restless children find the necessary level of concentration difficult to sustain. Some children may feel threatened by the themes and issues that are raised. Some will be emotionally and socially competent and others will find life much more difficult. Many will actively support what you are doing while others may appear disinterested.

Circle Time is an inclusive and democratic system where all children are encouraged to contribute as well and as much as they are able. It is sensitive to their different competencies and uses a range of strategies to ensure that every child benefits and comes away from each session with their self-esteem strengthened and their confidence raised.

Why are so many children fidgeting?	The pace may be too slow. You need to keep the children 'asking for more' so make sure that none of the games or activities are allowed to drag on. Keep the pace brisk and your children will stay alert.
Why do some children seem restless and anxious?	Are your expectations too high? Are you asking them to formulate sentences and ideas that are too complex or to recall, or to carry, too many pieces of information? Keep each plan simple. If an issue is complex, you need to break it down into small, manageable chunks and investigate them one at a time. A problem of bullying might be split into name-calling; pushing and shoving; where and when; how to respond. Each issue can then be dealt with in a separate session.
Some children have told me that Circle Time is boring. What am I doing wrong?	Your expectations may be too low and your meetings may have become routine. Circle Time meetings are democratic, so why don't you have round 'Circle Time would be better

if...?' Maybe they want to learn some new games? Maybe they want to use some new ways of holding the open forum?

What can I do to make sure that everyone feels motivated?	Are you sticking to your session plan too rigidly? Successful circle meetings require give-and-take. Make sure that you are responding to what is actually happening in the meeting. Be prepared to let go of the script and let the children decide how a meeting will progress.
What do I do about children who keep saying 'pass'?	They may be shy or unwilling, but they might also be finding the rounds too difficult. Simplify your rounds for a while to allow the children to get the hang of what is expected. Try prompts such as 'If I were an animal, I would be...' and similar fun rounds so that they can get used to making their contribution. Ask your adult helpers to sit next to shy children so that they can be given help. If you give them the 'sentence stem' in advance, older children can write their contribution on a scrap of paper and read it out. Don't forget puppets: they can chat to the children about what will happen in the meeting and offer to speak for any child who feels shy. He or she can then tell the puppet their sentence before the meeting and the puppet will repeat it at the appropriate time.

Children are not 'opening up'. What should I do?

Maybe your meetings have become too intrusive. Try using the more distanced approach of metaphor. Use stories and puppets so that the children can discuss the characters without being expected to refer everything to their own personal experiences.

Your class may not be ready to engage in deep discussion. You need to build the necessary levels of trust and group strength. Concentrate on games and activities that will build these into the group before you attempt to use the 'Opening up' phase for more difficult issues.

Focus on celebrating things that are going well and remember that not all meetings need to be about problem-solving.

I'm finding Circle Time very tiring. Am I trying too hard?

Are you trying to cover too much ground in each session? It is better to investigate one small issue thoroughly than to try to rush through many issues too quickly. Make sure that your meetings are timetabled when you are feeling fresh and energetic. Circle Time is too important to be squashed into a Friday afternoon or held at a time when you are not at your best.

Getting the room ready is sometimes difficult. What should I do?

Can older children get it ready for you? If not, you need to train your children so that it is a smooth-running drill. If you always have your meetings at the same time on the same day, this will soon become routine. Book the hall!

Children sometimes seem embarrassed. How do I prevent this?

Are you using your meetings to punish or complain about behaviour? If you do, you will make the whole group fearful that this week it will be their 'turn'. Never put the spotlight on individual children and what they are doing wrong. A circle meeting is not a courtroom or an opportunity for having a good moan. When you are planning you need to focus on your learning outcomes and remember that these are the emotional and social skills that you want your children to acquire.

The children don't seem to have many ideas. How can I help them?

Are you preparing them sufficiently? Try telling them what the meeting will be about a few days beforehand so they can make themselves ready. Make sure that you always hold your meetings on the same day and at the same time so that they know what to expect.

What can I do about a couple of attention-seeking children who keep ruining my Circle Times?

Try beating them at their own game by being more interesting and exciting than they are! Have surprises ready. You can forestall many problems by using diversionary tactics. Circle Time practitioners call this their 'bag of power'. It could be a puppet that is pulled from a bag at an opportune moment or a wand or rain-stick that can focus attention on you as the leader and away from the child who is trying to disrupt your meeting. Ensure that the pace of your meetings is upbeat and that you have planned plenty of activities – if the children are busy, you will find that opportunities for showing off are few.

There are always a few children who continually disruptive. What can I do to settle them down?

If a child is continually disruptive a visual warning can be used. Make a number of cards that have a sad face drawn on one side and a happy face on the other. Keep these cards handy so that you can place one beside the child who is spoiling the meeting. Tell her that the face is sad because she has made the whole group sad by breaking an important rule. If the child responds positively and begins to behave well, you can smile and turn the card over to show the happy face. Explain that everyone is now pleased with her. If the child is unable to change the behaviour, ask her to sit outside the circle and watch a one-minute sand-timer before asked if she is ready to rejoin the group.

I am worried a child might make a disclosure

Don't forget children may never mention anyone's name in a negative way. They have to say 'Someone is calling me names...' 'Some people are shouting at me...'. Also, prior to Circle Time, children should know they can have a one-to-one chat with you if ever anything personal is troubling them. At all times it is important that you remain calm and responsive and react with respect. You can divert the child from the 'issue' by focusing on their feelings. This means that the feeling can be named and shared and the child can see that other children have had the same feeling which, in turn, means that they feel less isolated and fearful. Show no alarm in your face – play games before they leave the circle and then quietly speak to the child afterwards.

Circle Time doesn't seem to make any difference to behaviour. What is going wrong?

Circle Time cannot work in a vacuum. It must reflect the values of your school. The behaviours that are taught during meetings must be praised and treasured during every minute of the school day. These behaviours and values must be modelled by all members of staff and need to be part of your school's values, rewards, sanctions and lunchtime systems.

I try to plan my own sessions but sometimes don't know where to begin. What can I do?

The purpose of circle meetings is to help children to learn essential emotional and social skills. What skills do your children need to learn? Once you have chosen the skill you want to teach, you need to find games and activities that will help your children learn those skills.

I want to involve the children in planning meetings so that the content is relevant. Is this a good idea?

Try a Circle Time suggestion box so that any pupil can contribute, anonymously, suggestions for themes that they want addressed in Circle Time.

Sometimes I feel that the children are too dependent on the praise they get from me in the celebration step of each meeting. How do I make them more independent?

Try to encourage children to nominate other children who are calm, create a lovely working atmosphere by not shouting out, or who are learning to walk away from fights and so on. Once they are nominated, if the majority of the class agree, the whole class can sign something called a 'Class Team Honours List'. If the child or the class don't feel they quite deserve the certificate yet, the child can place himself on an 'Achievement Ladder' at what they feel is the appropriate rung.

Circle Time meetings seem to lose their focus and start to ramble. How can I stop this?

This is a pace issue. Take control, move on to the next activity and never allow them to drag. Make sure that you have planned thoroughly but have your 'bag of power' ready for those emergencies when you can see that the children are not ready or willing to do as you planned.

Be Kind To Yourself!

Your mood affects the quality of all your interactions with children and staff. You need to look after yourself very carefully – your energy is the key to unlocking excellence in your classroom. Teachers always tend to put other people's needs first. It would be kinder to everyone if you put your own needs first! Try and do all the things that you know you should – give yourself time boundaries, eat good food, drink lots of water ... get to bed early! Most importantly though, during the day give yourself a 'Golden Moment' by rewarding yourself with small treats. Have a quiet moment with special music, a good coffee, tasty food and quietly reflect on how lucky we are to work with children. I know it sounds daft – but they are wise and funny and very courageous at times. If we don't become more relaxed and positive we will fail to see their great qualities.

Quality Circle Time has been developed by Jenny Mosley and her team over the past 20 years as a whole-school approach to enhancing self-esteem and, developing positive behaviour and relationships within the school community.
For more information visit our website
www.circle-time.co.uk

We love running training days for individuals, schools, clusters – everyone! Contact:

Jenny Mosley Consultancies
28A Gloucester Road
Trowbridge BA14 0AA
Tel: 01225 767157
Fax: 01225 755631
E-mail: circletime@jennymosley.co.uk

For a catalogue of exciting books and puppets published by Positive Press please contact:

Positive Press
28A Gloucester Road
Trowbridge BA14 0AA
Tel: 01225 719204
Fax: 01225 712187
E-mail: positivepress@jennymosley.co.uk

Anyone can download SEAL resources from **www.dfes.gov.uk**